RADICAL COMPASSION

Subverting a Culture of Hostility

Thad Cummings

RADICAL COMPASSION:
Subverting a Culture of Hostility

Copyright © 2019 Thad Cummings

All rights reserved.

ISBN: 978-0-9993850-4-3 (paperback)
ISBN: 978-0-9993850-5-0 (e-book)

Library of Congress Control Number: 2019902326

Cover Art Credit: Beth Winterburn–
Painting: *Blue No. 8*, www.BethWinterburn.com

Printed in the United States of America

A note from the author

I found myself half way into reading *Strength to Love* by Martin Luther King Jr and the words he wrote in 1963 could have just as easily been written in 2019, "Deep clouds of anxiety and depression are suspended in our mental skies. More people are emotionally disturbed today than at any other time in human history." Our country is more polarized than ever, the world seems to always be falling apart and we are more eager to make enemies with anyone who thinks differently than we do rather than show any form of remorse. Suffice it to say, compassion is the furthest thing from the conversation. I need to make it clear, I'm not interested in another 30-day quick fix book nor am I interested in surface level conversations that only look at symptoms while neglecting root causes. I'm interested in diving into the deep work and challenge all of our current viewpoints so that we may shift the dialogue, even in the slightest, to finding more joy in our lives and our relationships and healing this broken world.

There are three words you will see over and over again throughout this book: compassion, grace, and love. I will use them interchangeably while acknowledging they are unique in their own regard. However, it is my firm belief that you cannot engage compassion as a verb without having grace as a noun, and both stem from the same root source of love. For the sake of semantics, the goal of this book and a quote by one of my editors Caroline, "Compassion is grace with legs on it." My first book, *Running From Fear*, concluded with chapter 13 "Finding Grace." As the second book in the series, we will pick up where we left off and dive into what grace and compassion look like as a bigger picture. This is a book not just about reflections and discussions, but actions. We don't live static lives, so let's not allow our hearts and minds to become static as well.

As always, thank you for taking the time to join this journey with me. Your time is valuable and I am truly humbled that you're willing to spend some of it with me. While we won't agree on everything (what fun would that be?), my hope is that you find your heart just a bit more open and filled with the grace, compassion and love we all deserve.

Thad

Table of Contents

Can compassion change the world?
And if so, why hasn't it happened already?

Introduction

It was 2011 and my friend, Chris, had just returned from a mission trip in the mountain villages of Haiti. I was anxious to hear all about it as we set out for a hike on what felt like a perfect, spring, Michigan morning. I endured nearly five full minutes of small talk about our families and life before I interrupted and asked him to tell me about the trip. He hesitated, taking a few more steps before looking at me saying, "It wasn't what I expected." There was a tension in his voice, an unexpected fusion of pain and remorse as his eyes returned to the rocky path ahead of us. He went on to explain that this was a mission trip to serve the "poor," to try and help in one of the most impoverished areas in the world. After speaking for several minutes, Chris lifted his gaze again, but this time, with a hint of shame in his eyes. "I went there to have empathy for the poor, but the poor had empathy for me, for my lack of joy amongst all my riches. I thought I was going there to help save them, but they were the ones saving me..."

The crisp, spring morning suddenly felt heavy and the chorus of singing birds faded from my ears. How is it that humans in one of the world's poorest villages, ravaged with famine, crime, drugs, no access to clean water or medical supplies, filled with diseases and infections, without electricity and hardly any shelter, were the ones having empathy for my friend? My friend, who lives in luxury with all modern conveniences never worrying where the next meal will come from. "The sense of community they had, the joy they shared with me, they had hardly any food but tried to feed me before themselves; the gratitude was unlike anything I've ever witnessed," he said as his voice was shaking. "They were the ones taking care of me, not the other way around." One question was left suspended in the air between us – "What if it is me who is actually poor?"

Poor (adjective): lacking material possessions; small in worth.
                    – *Merriam Webster Dictionary*

What does it really mean to be "poor"? Is it just a matter of material possessions? Throughout this book, I would like to expand the definition of "poor" from a statement about economics and wealth and evolve it into many aspects of life. To begin with, I would split the definition into four main categories: financially poor, poor in health, poor in education and resources, and poor in life and spirituality. These categories can then be further broken down. For example, those who are poor in life or spirit may feel: relationally poor, poor of passion, poor of love, poor in purpose, poor in faith, etc. Now I'm not going to treat this like a textbook to cover each of the four categories with definitive examples in a succinct pattern; life does not work in neat categories. Instead, this conversation will unfold through a series of stories that engage and overlap each category. Before we begin, let's set the stage by redefining *poor* in a new light to open the conversation and challenge our own stories (no offense to Meriam-Webster).

Poor (adjective): lacking an element for wholeness in joy

Bluntly speaking, I think every person is poor in some regard and we have to look beyond the obvious physical signs to see it. Many of our lives are riddled with bouts of fear, anger, bitterness, jealousy, judgment, or resentment. While I believe these sources of pain and despair may be rooted in a place of fear, I think they also point to a large inadequacy in our lives – a shortage of joy. When life seems to be overflowing with joy and compassion, there is often little room to harbor any of this pain and despair. Yet most of us are consumed with the pain and despair to some degree. Why else would topics like greed and envy be so commonplace in society?

This book is about a change in perception of our "poorness." Instead of seeing it as a fault, there is a humbling power that our poorness has the capability to bind humanity on a level that turns inadequacies into gifts, weaknesses into strengths and delusions into a shared virtue of enlightenment. All of this comes from a shift in perspective where we realize two things:

we all have needs

&

we all have something to offer

Take the example of my friend visiting Haiti who went with physical resources such as medicine, food and building supplies to a village that desperately needed them. Absolutely wonderful. But in return, the village shared with him a compassion of grace, love and community that he was desperately searching for, and didn't even realize how much he yearned for it until it was bestowed upon him. We have the ability to fill in the gaps for one another. In fact, it is part of our purpose. It's how humanity was designed.

This shift in awareness is vital because on one hand, it keeps us from reverting to a characterization of victimhood where we believe we have nothing to offer this world. That mentality forces us to conclude we are powerless in our circumstances or even that our very presence is a statement of bad luck and a testament to the wake of damage we will inevitably leave behind for even trying. On the other hand, if we attempt to help another person without engaging from a place of empathy, or acknowledging we also have needs, it will leave our interactions with that person directional (or one sided). This approach allows barriers to stay in place and it allows us to keep ourselves at a distance, taking on God-complexes of superiority to say, "I have something you need and I choose where to give it."

We will discuss these trains of thought (and many more throughout the book) for these inadequate ways of thinking block the potential outcome of **cyclical compassion**. A new cycle that creates tangible change when we participate without asking, "What is in it for me?" and instead begin saying, "Here is what I can offer." Cyclical compassion opens the door for humility where we can simultaneously posture ourselves to accept love and grace in return. Our world view continues to grow as we see the positive feedback loop this cycle creates. It awakens us to issues like the pain, destruction, despair and loneliness created in our competitive efforts toward the futile labeled horizon of "success." Then, and only then, do we see that success in life is not about climbing a corporate ladder, accumulating wealth and possessions, or striving to be the best employee, athlete, student, family, fill in the _____.

No, the more our worldview expands, the more we realize the only competition that matters in this life is in living life to our fullest potential: a life full of grace and compassion for all of the "poor" in the world; including ourselves.

PART 1

CHANGING OUR POSTURE

"The more you connect with the poverty of another, the more you connect with your own poverty."
—*AJ Sherrill*

1

ROADBLOCKS TO COMPASSION:

acknowledging our hang-ups

*"The system isn't broken,
it was designed this way.
– Lisa Gungor*

Have you ever started a project, like putting together a piece of Ikea furniture, only to realize you had the wrong tools? Roadblocks are like having a hammer when you need a screwdriver. So before we can dive in, we need to discuss some of the roadblocks that can keep us from engaging the rest of the work in this book. This single chapter could encompass an entire book – in actuality, it could probably encompass multiple books. It's why Lisa Gungor's quote paralyzed me the first time I read it; we aren't breaking things, this is how the entire system was built, it's how we were taught to engage the world. The good news is if we can understand that, we can work to change the systems in place – we can fix them. For the sake of moving on to further material, I'd like to simplify this conversation by focusing on three major types of roadblocks that I think we can all relate to and let you unfold the rest in your own discernments.

#1) Fearful doubt: "What if I'm wrong?"

If purgatory exists, it's known here on earth as the intensive care unit (ICU). I was in Utah with my stepfather visiting his son, Kris, in the hospital. ICUs are stressful places and you are never visiting one because a friend or family member is doing "well" by any definition. Aside from an operating table, it is the most serious place a person can be within the hospital. Kris had a stroke of bad luck in his childhood when a virus went to his heart. The damage was permanent and irreversible. Although Kris did his best to stay as healthy and active as possible, 30 years later he would find himself battling a flu he just couldn't shake. He was dropped off at the local emergency room and upon entering the hospital he collapsed as his heart stopped beating not once, but twice. A week, a day, an hour earlier, anything short of him walking into the hospital and he would not be alive. I did my best to convey to his father what he was about to see, but nothing can prepare a father to see his son connected to a dozen machines including ECMO, a machine that was beating for Kris's heart. Conversations take on a whole new meaning when you can't speak to your child who has multiple tubes down his throat breathing for him. Dialogue was limited to what energy Kris could muster up to write fragmented sentences on a piece of paper.

An awkward dance exists when you aren't prepared for the situation and you don't remotely know how the person lying in the hospital bed is holding up apart from being terrified and miserable. Small talk doesn't exist even though you try your best to force it in order to rationalize some form of calm. Kris's skin was pale-white in contrast to the garden hose size tubes of deep burgundy carrying his life back and forth to the machine. His body was covered in lines and wires, his eyes were so heavy as though they aged 10 years from the last time I saw him. Walking up to the bedside, I froze. I didn't know what to say to my brother, I didn't know what to say to my stepfather, I didn't know what to say, period. I just stood there trying my best not to add to the chaos of the moment and force a smile for fear of shedding a tear.

The nurse came back to administer medication so I took that as my cue to leave. I returned to the waiting room to clear my head and stared out the window at the mountains. A voice broke my concentration as I turned to see a woman with long black hair talking on a cell phone. You can always tell the distinct difference between the people who are visiting the hospital for the first time and those who have been living in the waiting room with the bad food, cheap lights and uncomfortable furniture coupled with stress beyond description. I overheard her conversation and watched as she broke tragic news to a sibling over the phone. She collapsed to the floor, sobbing hysterically. I didn't ask her if she was ok or if she needed anything, I didn't offer a shoulder to cry on, I just stood there watching, entrenched in an isolated state of chaos and confusion.

I wanted to reach out a hand, to say something, *anything*, but my mind began to race: What if she wants to be left alone? What if she gets mad at me for asking? What if she just needs space?

Sure, but what if I'm wrong?

What if she just lost her partner, what if her world just collapsed, what if she wants to know for only a moment that she isn't alone, that someone else cares, that someone else is willing to sit and share that pain? What if she too was staring out at the mountains only moments before wondering if it was all real?

The air felt stifling.
Life is heavy like that sometimes.

We've all had those moments when we are hurt or angry or frustrated with life and we just want to be left alone. To an extent, I don't think there is anything wrong with that. Sometimes it's necessary to blow off some steam and think things through on our own. In the long term, however, it can become a dangerous strategy: a thinly veiled excuse to keep us at arm's length from the world. Yet often, it is ironically those same moments when we are desperate to feel anything *but* alone in this world. When we encounter another person who is going through difficulties, we might subconsciously project our insecurities onto them, particularly to make sure we avoid an awkward or uncomfortable situation. We'd like to think that perhaps they are fine or don't need help or would prefer to be left alone just like us (and why risk the opportunity of being wrong to find out otherwise?). I think we take this notion of being "wrong" and apply it too liberally, allowing it to keep us from touching the idea of compassion altogether. Our response has consequences; it's like donning armor to protect yourself from others, only to find that there are spikes on the inside piercing you instead.

While we've all been in such a situation, this "armor" or "cage" can feel intangible and difficult to discern. Putting it in context, we might realize how this notion of being "wrong" can actually be used in reverse to eliminate this roadblock entirely.

To be clear, this isn't a conversation limited to big events in hospital waiting rooms. Loneliness, despair and isolation are real and everywhere. According to the American Foundation for Suicide Prevention, there is an average of 121 suicides per day amounting to 44,193 deaths per year. It is the 10th leading cause of death in the United States. And for every successful attempt, there are 25 failed attempts. That's over 1.1 million suicide attempts per year just in the United Sates. Most of us know at least one person who has been affected by suicide, but let's take this one step further. According to the Anxiety and Depression Association of America, over 40 million Americans battle with anxiety and depression on a daily basis. Loneliness, despair and isolation have touched every one of us.

That's just as heavy to say out loud.

I know these statistics not because I researched them on Google. I know them because I've experienced them personally and have seen or heard a similar experience in just about every relationship in my life. Why, then, didn't I reach out to ask that woman if she was ok? Why couldn't I look my brother in the eyes? Why didn't I say anything to my stepfather? Those are the initial questions and they open the floodgates to many more. Remember, this isn't just a conversation about a person poor in health. Why do I briskly walk past a homeless person who is asking for money? Why do I avoid making eye contact with the person sitting silently on the bus staring at the floor? Why don't I say *thank you* to the person taking out the trash at the office building or ask the mother of three if she needs a hand with her groceries – especially as the youngest begins to have a meltdown in the checkout aisle?

Why can I be so engaging with compassion one day, and then complacent, or standoffish the next? Dennis Van Kampen, the president of Mel Trotter Ministries for the homeless said, "People do not become homeless from a lack of money, they become homeless due to a lack of relationships." I feel like this statement starts to shed some light enabling us to have this conversation with an illuminated perspective that applies to all aspects of compassion in our lives. Compassion is one of the most in-depth elements of a relationship we can have with another and with ourselves. This notion of being wrong—feeding our doubt in what we have to offer and to give—is significant in and of itself and it ties right into what I find to be the most common roadblock to compassion.

#2 Convenient Compassion: "Is this easy and agreeable for me?"

I have had a million excuses to keep me at bay when it comes to practicing compassion. It's not to say I'm not full of compassion; it's just that compassion feels more or less accessible when it is convenient for me. When my day is going well, I'm rested, I'm caught up on my to-do list, my hair looks good and my new shoes fit just right, of course I'm happy to help then! But how often does that happen? What about when I am indeed tired, exhausted, frustrated, furious, behind, really behind, late, or extremely late? Don't even get me started if I have a personal feud with you. Under any of these circumstances I suddenly have a whole new set of questions and standards that enable me to avoid compassion. I'm not talking about the obvious questions like what if I'm more late or what if this makes me fall even more behind... no, those make me sound selfish so I have newer and more preferred questions I can ask that make it better for <u>them</u> that I don't get involved: What if that person isn't struggling? What if they are offended by me asking? What if they think I'm a creep or a jerk? What if I embarrass them? What if they embarrass me? What if I say something wrong? What if I cause a scene? What if they say "no" or laugh in my face?

Sure, but what if I'm wrong?

What if that person has no one left? What if no one has reached out and asked them how they are doing? What if they haven't heard that they are loved or that they matter or that they have worth in *days*, or *months* or even *years*? What if they just want someone to talk to, someone to say it is going to be ok or someone to tell them they aren't crazy or alone?

The truth is, I'm not a genie, I don't know every circumstance and story to tell you when to engage and when not to. I've been rejected lots of times when reaching out and sometimes I've been embarrassed by it. But those times are actually few and far between. When it turns out I was indeed wrong and that person did need a friend, I can't begin to tell you the amazing experiences and friendships, even if only momentary, that have come from those pivotal moments. And how? All because I took a chance and stepped outside my comfort zone leaving my pitiful excuses behind.

Are you ready for the most frustrating part?

Offering compassion isn't going to happen conveniently for you just like there is never a convenient time for that bad or earth-shattering thing to happen in the first place. Who has ever offered condolences for the death of a pet and that owner responds, "Oh not to worry, it was a convenient time for Sparky to die." No form of pain in your life happens at a convenient time and your compassion should not be predicated on convenience either.

Yes, it will interrupt your perfectly planned week. It will come at 3 a.m. while you are sick in bed with the flu. It will come during that work meeting when you're trying so hard to get a promotion. It will come when your kid is throwing a tantrum and it will most certainly come in the middle of that Big Ten football game you've been waiting weeks to see. I'm sorry, but life doesn't care even if the game just went into overtime. And if you're married to someone who loves sports, I give you full permission to read that out loud to them. Or swap the word "game" for; Netflix, workout, party, concert, naptime, or however else you'd like to fill in the blank.

#3 Judgment: "Do they deserve compassion?"

This is by far the hardest to discuss. In fact, I knew it would be easier if I left it out in the hopes that you might skim past this section without bringing it up. Nevertheless, we have to discuss it. I can't throw any cheesy one-liners out there to make this one palatable and it runs much deeper than interrupting any football game. In fact, compassion is oftentimes easier when it is a stranger and there is no baggage or history attached. But as I discussed in my book, *Running From Fear*, hurt people hurt people. One major indicator of moving through the forgiveness process is the ability to have compassion on those whom you would have previously deemed "unworthy of your grace," by acknowledging the pain they are carrying. This isn't effortless, it takes time, and it is something we will return to throughout this book.

To reframe this last point with some context, have you ever made a mistake or hurt someone? Would you want them to forgive you? The answer to both of these questions should be nothing short of "yes and yes."

I'll open up the confession box and admit that I've battled bouts of depression many times. I've also done and said things to the point where I struggled to grasp whether or not I deserved compassion. If we are all being completely honest, I think most of us have battled serious issues of doubts, loneliness, anger, funks, or resentment in our lives, all but lashing out at the heavens to scream "Why!?" But sometimes, the desire to take another step beyond questions like, "Should I keep going?" or "What is even the point to all of this?" comes not from within, but from another person. Not necessarily a person who shared some wisdom or had some answer for us, but a friend, a lover, a stranger: someone who was simply present in a difficult time. Who reminds us that we are loved. Who helps us see that we all make mistakes and we aren't actually alone in this world no matter how hard that can feel at times. Most importantly, this is someone who takes time to notice and genuinely cares: someone whose compassion isn't constrained by conveniences, by the fear of being wrong, or by determining if you deserve it or not.

This chapter isn't limited to only these three road-blocks. We can come up with plenty of excuses and road-blocks every day to avoid having compassion. I get it, life is hard, we get tired, we get behind, sometimes we just can't. But I want to argue something different here. Compassion isn't just something you work toward or a nice afterthought that occurs if you have time.

Compassion is the source of vitality in this life.

Compassion takes on more power than any other entity. It's a means to stop unnecessary suffering. It's a step toward ending the tragic statistics of depression and suicide of people poor in life, a step toward visiting that person in the hospital who is poor in health, a step toward supporting a group of persons in Haiti who have no resources and a step toward building a relationship with a person who may be penniless and homeless.

For all of my friends out there thinking you don't have a compassionate bone in your body, I want to make it clear that compassion isn't just a necessary component of life nor an elusive trait of selfless servers and non-profits.

Compassion is in all of us at the core of our being.

We already have it because it is the fundamental basis to the very essence of who we truly are. We are born of compassion and we can only exist in this life through the substance of compassion. Sometimes we just have to change our vantage point in order to see this, as well as believe it. That's what this discussion is ultimately about: a change in perspective.

If you don't believe in this for one reason or another, that is ok. I fought this reality for years. But I still want to challenge you to read this book from a place of openness and to consider one vital train of thought:

> *What if it could be true, that compassion is the essence of my existence, and how would that viewpoint change my outlook on life?*

The first part of this book is a conversation meant to expose us to the possibility that compassion is an indisputable and innate truth. I will challenge you to see new perspectives to overcome your roadblocks to compassion and to see different aspects of the poorness we are all facing. The second half of the book will help us find ways to put compassion into action so it is no longer a pleasant afterthought for a bumper sticker, but an actual, tangible, concrete aspect of our daily actions. Ready for a ride? I promise it will be worth it.

Let's journey together.

CHAPTER 1 NOTES AND REFLECTIONS

In what areas of your life (finances, spiritual life, resources, or health) would you consider yourself poor? What roadblocks keep you from engaging compassion for yourself or from offering it to others? In what ways do you currently find yourself offering compassion to yourself or to others?

_____

_____

_____

_____

_____

_____

_____

_____

_____

_____

2

GIVING YOURSELF GRACE:

it's time to let go of the competition and your past

> *"If you want to live a life you've never lived, you have to do things you've never done."*
> – Jen Sincero

If we cannot give ourselves grace, then how are we ever going to be able to receive grace?

If we cannot receive grace, then how are we ever going to be able to give grace to others?

For many years, my life's goal was to simply serve anyone and everyone. Don't go trying to paint me as a saint just yet; this is a two-sided coin kind of story. One side of my reasoning came from a place that was genuine and heartfelt, but the other side was escaping the pain from my past. I wanted to help people, but *why* I was helping them was a matter that danced around a gray line. Of course I received something from serving others. I think it's safe to say there is a level of gratification we all get from making the day or easing the burden of another, not to mention it is a simple way to attest that we matter in this chaotic world. In my case, I was unfortunately dependent upon that outward evidence of value. My worth was dependent upon what others gave me and this is where things get obscured... kind of like posting something on Facebook or Instagram and waiting to see how many likes you'd get. Planting community gardens in food desert areas, building filters for families in Kenya, cooking meals for the homeless youth center, clearing invasive species from the local forest, you name it: I did anything I could do to prove I was going to make a difference. It was a competition with the rest of the world when I was really only playing against myself.

Again, it is not "what" I was doing, it was my reasoning, the "why" I was doing it in the first place that was off. To word this differently, if you're too busy realizing how amazing I am, then that doesn't leave much room for discovering all of my flaws and insecurities. We all have unique ways in which we respond to determining our worth and value. It follows this belief that if you only knew who I was, the real me, that might not be good enough. Or you might condemn me for those flaws and insecurities. This fear is deeply ingrained and sourced from two forces in our lives that are keeping us from offering grace to ourselves: societal influences and our own belief in our unworthiness (and both of these tend to feed off of each other). I want to spend more time in this chapter breaking down both forces since the rest of our work will be futile if we cannot first offer ourselves grace. To begin, I want to step back and look at it from the context of society for just a moment.

Our ancestral roots, for example, have a dark history that desired, longed for, and loved to bear witness to atrocities like beheadings, hangings, stonings, and crucifixions. Forget the notion of pain for a moment; these ordeals were meant to be publicly humiliating... to completely shatter a person's worth for the world to see and cast their judgments upon. These are no longer legal forms of punishment in this country, so instead we have easy access to platforms like social media to get our fix for public shaming. Social media has its positive aspects, I know, but much of this new-found access to judgment is nothing short of an epidemic. It took the power from the emperors and sheriffs of the olden days and put it into the hands of anyone with an electronic rectangle in their pocket. Now we all have the capacity to be healers and forgivers or accusers and executioners at our fingertips. Sadly, we often lean toward the accuser over the forgiver and that has real consequences for our ability to have grace on ourselves. This is especially potent if other people reinforce a narrative that we are not deserving of grace.

Personally, I can't stand it when people don't like me. Especially when people find a flaw in me to exploit, judge, or condemn (not that I know anyone who does enjoy it). I take it personally from people who don't even know me. That said, it only seems natural to now share one of my worst moments of public humiliation and defeat because it single handedly collapsed my ability to even think about the idea of grace or compassion for months.

It was Monday morning and I was heading out to lock up a farm-to-table restaurant I had purchased earlier that year. Standing at the front door, I twisted the key over and over again until I heard the distinct metal clink when the dead bolt released. It was only 11 a.m. but the sky was riddled with dark clouds and the wind was bitterly cold against my bare hands. I remember every detail of it because that dreary November day would be the last time I'd hear the sound of that metal clink. It was the day my restaurant would shut down for good. It was the day I lost my desire to (and belief that I could) make any long-term impact in my community.

I couldn't quite come to terms with how this happened. In only a few short months after purchasing the place, I took a bankrupt business swimming in debt and morphed it into a profitable enterprise. Over the next nine months, my team and I withstood food shortages, employee shortages, customer shortages, equipment shortages and everything that could go wrong in running a restaurant. Employees cursed at me in front of customers, hood vents caught on fire, people I tried to help consistently stole money, we even had one gentleman break in and take the entire register once! We overcame so many obstacles including the countless mistakes I made being new to ever owning a restaurant, but in the end, the restaurant couldn't financially survive hit after hit after hit. I was physically and emotionally exhausted.

The biggest regret I had when the doors closed was not losing all the money, it was shutting down my community food program. A program where we could supply local, organic, healthy meals for free to our community. It was a bit ironic that when I realized the end was only weeks away, I was notified that I would be receiving an award for the "Brightest and Most Sustainable Business of the Year" for our work in the community. Needless to say, I didn't even show up for my acceptance speech. I was embarrassed because of my personal failure and because of all the people I let down. But that didn't matter in the public eye. One of the first newspaper articles released touted me as "another failed social enterprise." That wasn't just the tip of the iceberg, it was the calving event that would open the floodgates to the hate mail I would ultimately receive.

There is this phone app for Facebook messages called Messenger where people who don't even know you can send a message that you can either reject or accept. One message (one of the less hateful messages I received) sits in the waiting queue that, to this day, I haven't deleted; it says, "Dumb Socialist. I am glad you are BROKE." These people didn't know me, who I was, my story, or why I was trying to do what I did, but they had no remorse for privately or publicly tarnishing anything and everything about me. No one was calling and asking if any of it was true, what happened, how I was doing, what I longed for or what I was trying to accomplish. It was my turn at the chopping block and for the next couple of weeks people were waiting in line to throw tomatoes at my face, metaphorically, or bricks through my window... literally.

At the time, I couldn't brush it off. It made me question my ability to even help people in the first place; it was like an acid burning away the part of my soul that longed to serve this world and I was not mentally prepared for its corrosive powers. It took months for me to consider the thought of volunteering or helping my community again. Months to face the narratives and redefine a new one based on who I am, not on what others perceived me to be. Eventually I was able to find the desire to serve again. Still, that message sits in my phone two years later as a reminder of this battle I am continually bumping up against. A battle to not only question everything I see and hear elsewhere, but a battle to keep a close watch on how I am defining my worth and value, especially when it comes to offering myself grace.

I often refer back to Don Miguel Ruiz's book, *The Four Agreements*, when he talks about our ability to communicate as one of the greatest gifts we humans have. Sadly, we often abuse and misuse this gift. He states, "But like a sword with two edges, your word can create the most beautiful dream, or your word can destroy everything around you." Hitler brought the entire world to its knees through the power of his word simply by preying on the fears and insecurities of others. It makes me reflect on how many times I've used my words to inflict pain into the lives of others. Do you ever take time to reflect on that? How many times in your life have you used your words to intentionally hurt someone, to talk gossip, or judge and criticize when you don't even know the whole story? These reflections cause me to pause and realize not only how I've spread agony into my community, but how I actually internalize the unhelpful words other people have chastised me with.

When your worth or value depends on others and how they respond to you, view you, engage with you, or think about you, you are hopelessly running on a hamster wheel going nowhere fast. They may love you now... but the minute you make a single mistake, they are waiting for you with pitchforks and torches in hand. It is a volatile, turbulent ride and I believe most of us are riding this rollercoaster due to our choice to look through society's lens to find our worth. But this isn't limited to our feverous desire to hold the power of judgment and shaming when people make mistakes. Our longing for societal acceptance is just as powerful, to stay out of the crosshairs of what I would call the "less than" category.

Living in the most powerful country in the world has trickle-down effects. Or maybe it's just human nature. Whatever the case, we long to be #1 whether we like to admit it or not. We don't want to be less smart, wealthy, popular, successful, strong, attractive, or _____, than anyone else, no matter the cost. From those of us who constantly seek the attention and affection of others for reassurance to those who pride themselves on not caring what others think, it is still a universal purpose. It seems counter-intuitive, but those who are independent, wealthy or influential are still susceptible to finding their value on the basis of another's opinions.

Why are many of us attracted to people who dress lavishly, own big houses, drive nice cars, and take fancy vacations? Perhaps it explains our draw to the exotic – we look to people who we might deem cultured for traveling the world, who have outlandish careers and life experiences, wild stories of adventures; these are the tales we fantasize over in movies and Instagram posts. What an ego boost for them! You see, whether through approval or in avoiding judgment, we base our worthiness on the fractured flaws of everyone else's opinions. We are allowing others to determine whether we deserve grace based on how cool, sexy, rich, influential, exotic or successful we may or may not appear to be.

Let me be more blunt. We have an addiction to platforms like social media, yes, but it's a larger issue than that. We face a cultural addiction. It's not just about getting the right selfie for our profile picture or the right sunset shot for our Instagram. It has evolved to the way we carry ourselves in our work or how we engage with friends and family dating back to the post World War II era of "keeping up with the Jones's." Before, we had a cultural addiction of trying to keep up with everyone; now, we attempt to one-up everyone. Uniqueness and being on top have now become the goal. Being unique is not necessarily a bad thing; it's when we want to look and perceive ourselves as being so unique that we inadvertently feel superior to others... that is when things start to fall apart.

We begin to lose our true uniqueness rooted in the depths of our soul, sacrificing this in order to create a new image with a higher altitude. When we are on "top," it means everyone is looking up at us trying to catch up. It is easy not only to judge, but to get value when people are drooling at your feet to hear what story you are going to share next or when someone asks you where you bought that dress. It makes us feel special, a temporary high, that becomes an addiction because we need to buy crazier, cuter outfits so as to never be seen wearing the same thing twice. Or we need to make even more money to buy an even bigger home and go on an even nicer vacation to find an even bigger adventure to tell an even bigger story. But what does this all mean to us? What does this mean to you and your wellbeing?

Toxic overload.

Giving yourself grace begins by releasing yourself from the societal comparison game of life. Your worth in life is not dependent upon having the latest BMW or visiting the rarest places in the world to have a good tale to share at dinnertime. It is not dependent upon what Darrel or Suzie think about your political views. Your worth is based on the reality that you are enough, just the way you are, regardless of what you own, where you live, what you do, how you dress, what you've accomplished, or where you've been. The rest is just a show and these performances we play can fade as quickly as the lights do when people move on to watch a new act from the *next* latest and greatest.

Also, we need to be cognizant of how we tend to carry these actions into the way we engage with others. It is not only about releasing yourself from the pressure of putting on a solo-act-performance of perfection, but how you bring that performance into your relationships. Having the nicest landscaping does not make you the best neighbor on the block. Buying your partner a bigger diamond does not make you a better husband. Throwing your kids elaborate parties does not make you a better parent. And just because you gave him flowers one time does not make you a better friend.

It is hopeless to have external compassion from a place of genuine authenticity if you cannot first give yourself grace. Especially if you are having compassion, not from a place of gratitude, but in an attempt to keep your altitude in the societal comparison game. Let's pick on the flower example for an easy target. It looks great on the outside but what's going on beneath the surface? How is that relationship really doing? Giving someone flowers after an argument is wonderful, except when it is used to avoid facing a potential mistake. My stepfather loves to reference forgive and forget as "water over the dam." Great in theory, but it hardly ever works. A quick fix usually means we are simply suppressing, dismissing, or evading confrontation by avoiding the issues at hand and the role we played in it. It allows us to walk away quicker and easier which doesn't leave much space for long-term resolution in offering yourself or the other person grace. Metaphorically speaking, giving flowers is a quick and effortless patch job that will last about a week before they end up in the compost pile out back.

We must take the issues deeper in order to under-stand, as well as resolve them. So forget the flowers, the landscaping and diamonds and birthday parties. We must engage our partner to know and love them well, as is true for our neighbors, our children, and our friends. However, none of this is possible if we aren't able to engage and love ourselves well – to step away from the games and root ourselves in the healing power of grace.

We all make mistakes, it is true, but we have to acknowledge this out loud, to ourselves and to those around us. *You cannot forgive yourself if you do not know what you are forgiving yourself for.* And you cannot know what you are forgiving yourself for if you do not sit with the mistakes you have made and see what they have to teach you. It's the only way to keep from repeating them over and over again. We have to change our posture to a place of forgiveness because we can only forgive others as much as we have forgiven ourselves. We can only love others as much as we love ourselves. And we can only journey with others as far as we have journeyed with ourselves. This is where our pursuit of compassion begins. Where our flowers can evolve into a sign of gratitude rather than a Walmart-special-plea for forgiveness. Don't miss an opportunity and let the water flow over the dam.

While it can be easier to discuss external obstacles like societal comparisons, avoiding shame and guilt, or how we define our worth and value, the conversation will be null and void if we do not begin to discuss the largest obstacle to this work: *ourselves.* We all carry stories of deep pain or everyday mistakes that make it seemingly impossible to have grace on ourselves. I'd like to wrap this chapter up by sharing two stories that give testament to the breadth of the spectrum this relates to. No matter where you fall on the scale, my goal is to show you the dire need to start this work with giving yourself grace.

Garry was an acquaintance; he ran a restaurant group that I supplied compostable to-go ware for from my first business. We spoke mostly in passing and chit chatted over zero-waste events I would help organize for them. Then through a mutual friend, I heard he had lost his daughter Mackenzie. I reached out to ask if we could get coffee sometime to see how he was doing and to learn more about her story. The pain behind losing his child made for an incredibly piercing conversation but the guilt and shame he carried for not spending more time with her before she passed just added to it. When Garry's wife was pregnant with Mackenzie, they found out their child would have one of four conditions: two meant she would not survive birth, two meant she would be born with either Down syndrome or Turner syndrome. Garry said he was depressed for weeks until the doctor called Christmas Eve to break the news; Mackenzie would be born with Down Syndrome, and the family erupted in jubilee.

This took me back a bit. Why on earth would one celebrate Down Syndrome? Garry lifted his head and answered my question before I could ask, "My daughter was going to live." But it wasn't a painless journey as she would be constantly tested by health crisis after health crisis. Seven years of memories, seven years of dancing and laughter and all of the joy Mackenzie brought into this world would be cut short by a virus that would make you or me lie on the couch for a couple days endlessly complaining that we didn't feel good. She had a compromised immune system. How was that fair? On top of all of the health complications she endured, on top of the physical, mental and cultural struggles faced through Down Syndrome and everything the family had gone through; how was any of this fair? The weight of his voice... His tears... I naively wanted to lift the world off his shoulders, even if only for a moment. Consumed by grief, Garry could not muster the strength to love himself beyond the shame and guilt that plagued his thoughts. He was physically and mentally incapable of having any form of compassion or grace on himself – a man who worked tirelessly to provide for his family so that kids like Mackenzie have a place in this world.

A few weeks later, Garry and I would volunteer together at Bethesda Farm, a therapeutic day program facility for adults with mental or physical disabilities. As we cleaned a horse stall, Garry looked around pondering out loud the life his daughter would have had at a place like this had she been able to live into adulthood. I felt so blessed to share that moment with Garry because I did not see the death of Mackenzie, I saw the love she taught Garry that was now pouring out into the community for others just like her, others who would be hardly noticed in our society. And that is the beautiful thing about compassion; it can sneak up on you when you least expect, when you don't even notice it is happening, and even if only temporary, there is a sigh of relief from all the pain this life gives us.

Garry's story comes with a pain I will never be able to articulate in words, but we all have moments when having compassion feels impossible and we tend to carry that around with us wherever we go. I remember reading author Gabrielle Bernstein's book, *May Cause Miracles,* and one of the challenges was to look yourself in the mirror and say, "I love you." I felt so uncomfortable I could barely make eye contact with myself and for the first two dozen times I could hardly do it without laughing, thinking about how ridiculous this was. Failing that simple exercise is one of the main narratives that prevents us from living a life abounding in grace. Take The Golden Rule for example – it is one of the first lessons we are taught in life: Treat others as you want to be treated.

In church, I was taught as a kid to "love your neighbor as you love yourself." I think we somehow tend to skip over the "yourself" part in both of these life lessons. Our harshest critics tend to come from within after we make mistakes, and we don't go easy on ourselves.

Years before meeting Garry, I was a regional sales manager for World Centric. I helped businesses of all shapes and sizes become more sustainable through the use of compostable (plant based) products like plates, cups and cutlery (alternatives to products such as Styrofoam cups at coffee shops). After driving ten hours through the night in a Midwest blizzard to attend a conference three states away, it's safe to say I was cold, exhausted and a bit on edge. It was one of those never-ending, "am I going to make it?", white-knuckle drives. I arrived with thirty minutes to spare and began to set up my booth to display my products to all of the incoming vendors. I returned to my car to get my box of samples, opened my trunk, and to my surprise there was no box, no samples, no marketing materials, nothing. Pretty hard to convince people to buy your product without so much as a picture of what your product is. I called myself every name in the book, screaming on the inside while trying not to draw attention to myself as the crazy person standing in the Holiday Inn parking lot. "Worthless pile of scum" would be a polite way of saying

how I labeled myself that freezing Wednesday morning. It's almost comical to think about it now, I was selling coffee cups for crying out loud, but it was certainly
earth-shattering at the time. How was I treating myself
any differently than those strangers treated me when
the restaurant shut down?

The next time you make a fairly decent mistake, get
frustrated and start laying into yourself, write it down,
get it all out and put it aside. After several days when
things have calmed down and the moment has passed, go
back and read what you wrote. Ask yourself if you would
say that to a co-worker, a friend, a spouse or your child?
What did that ultimately accomplish and how big of a
mistake was it in the grand scheme of things? Are you
using your words to create a beautiful dream or destroy
everything around you?

I share these stories because from the simple mistakes to the deepest despair in life, we don't tend to go
easy on ourselves. Or we let our past mistakes define
who we are in the present. It is imperative that we dis-
sect both the external as well as the internal voices that
keep us from having grace and compassion on ourselves.
It has taken years, but I'm beginning to not only understand both sides of my own coin but also to alter my
"why." I continue to long to serve in my community and

the more grace I've been able to have on myself, the less my baggage comes with me in my acts of service. The less it becomes about determining my worth or what others may think, and instead, I find myself more capable to share that grace with those I encounter.

Step one in our journey begins with having grace and compassion on ourselves for all the mistakes that we have made in the past, make today, and will continue to make in the future. This includes all of those seemingly insignificant mistakes that accumulate throughout the week to the deep regrets that haunt our dreams. Grace is how we can grow and learn from these mistakes so that they are no longer defining us. Compassion is how we can grow to have a love that we cannot contain within ourselves and must share it back with others. Once we can begin to have grace and compassion on ourselves, it is then, and only then, that we can begin to receive grace and compassion *from* others.

CHAPTER 2 NOTES AND REFLECTIONS

How do you contend with yourself after making a small or large mistake? In what ways do you picture giving yourself grace? What past mistakes are still defining who you are in the present? What societal comparisons are keeping you from being you? How are you using your words to build dreams or destroy everything around you?

_____

_____

_____

_____

_____

_____

_____

_____

_____

_____

3

RECEIVING GRACE:

engaging vulnerability and humility

"What we do comes out of who we believe we are."
– Rob Bell

H ave you ever found yourself shaking and sweating profusely as you stand in front of a group of people ready to deliver a speech... only to forget what you were going to say? Thanks to my businesses, I was used to speaking in front of crowds, but I was an expert in those topics. I could talk to you all day about recycling, zero-waste, energy reduction, sustainability; topics I could master. This was different. You can't necessarily become an expert in topics like humility and vulnerability since they don't have scientific equations you can just solve or put into neat parameters. It's not something they teach you in school or college; there's no Humility 101 class. When I first stepped onto that stage to speak about these topics, doubt knifed me mercilessly – "Who am I to be speaking about any of this? How did I go from a safe, comfortable life, to starting over in an emotional frontier that can't be conquered or solved?"

Yet, on the other hand, who am I not to? I am always amazed when I trace back the moments that led to radical changes in my life. Steve Jobs gave a commencement speech to Stanford's graduating class of 2005, telling them:

"You can't connect the dots looking forward; you can only connect them looking backwards. So you have to trust that the dots will somehow connect in your future. You have to trust in something—your gut, destiny, life, karma, whatever. This approach has never let me down, and it has made all the difference in my life."

[As a side note, take the time to be retrospective. I encourage you to look back and see if you can't connect the dots in your life. Start with an obvious example like, what you do for a living, and then trace back all of the steps that led you to taking that career. Then move into deeper questions about how you discovered your joys and passions.]

The year leading up to my debut public speech on vulnerability and humility, a group of folks from my church started gathering regularly on Sunday evenings for dinner. It seemed like a picture-perfect gathering of friends, parents and kids living in harmony over freshly baked cornbread and pumpkin pie. During one dinner, my friend Ryan asked if anyone would like to share a thought with the group next time, so the following gathering I wrote up what would come to be known as, "Thad Talks." Five minutes of me sharing insights in my first public display of open honesty. I would share parts of my current struggles and past mistakes, things I had learned, and some thoughts on taking next steps. These talks were nothing earth shattering or grandiose, but they actually enabled me to begin tackling my first book because I realized how such topics shifted the dynamics of conversation within the group. People weren't looking for an expert, they were looking for somebody to start the conversation.

I didn't realize it at the time, but I was unintentionally engaging my stories from a place of vulnerability and humility. Typically, I would do everything in my power to hide my flaws and insecurities, not to admit them out loud (let alone in front of a group!). It was much easier to avoid the pain from the past and the ways in which I am flawed; why on earth would I reveal that in a public forum? Humility wasn't simple at first because I found myself not talking about how I had figured things out, but how many mistakes I had made and how much I really managed to make a mess out of things.

The early talks were nerve-wracking and I remember my first one like it was yesterday. The topic was about the idea of surrender. I threw the question out to the group, "What do you need to surrender to in order to be set free?" Why? Because my life was in shambles and there was so much of my past that I was still clinging to, attempting to salvage, but I could sense and feel this new pull. A draw toward new life. I was embarrassed to be so imperfect, I was embarrassed at the person I had been, and, in many ways, still was. But after the talks were finished and my nerves calmed down, I always paid attention to those subtle shifts in the conversation of the group. As it turns out, this wasn't a picture-perfect group and I was not the sour apple holding it back from "really blossoming." Everyone had sour apples in their pocket and each week it seemed like a new story with a new person or family would unfold. Struggles with infertility, marriage, illnesses, kids, mistakes, and all matters of obstacles in life. There is a beautiful gift that comes from the reality of interconnectedness through the resounding humility of imperfection. When we can engage our relationships from a place of authenticity and admit that we are struggling, we create a safe place for others to say, "me too." This is how true compassion grows.

When we are candid enough to admit that we don't have it all figured out, that we cannot do it alone and we indeed need help – even if that help is simply emotional presence – we allow others to engage our pain and have empathy for us. Not from a place of inferiority or superiority, but from a place of equality. Honestly, much of my life and my relationships were affected by the notion of "If only they knew." For instance, people might thank me for something and I would be crawling in my skin, mumbling under my breath, "You don't know me, you don't know all of the mistakes I've made, because if you did, you surely wouldn't be thanking me."

I couldn't shake it off. It was like an old CD that was scratched and would get stuck on repeat in the car stereo. When people would tell me that they'd keep me in their thoughts, or worse, ask if they could pray for me, I'd be counting down the seconds until I could get out the front door (or even better, quietly escape out the back). It wasn't because I didn't appreciate their heartfelt sincerity. I simply and genuinely didn't believe I was worthy of it. As it turns out, most people I've met struggle to define their worth and value. Perhaps you can start to see why it is so important that we redefine "enough?" If we do not believe we are worthy of grace, we cannot receive grace well. We regress to building another road block to deflect any possibility of humility and forgiveness people may offer us. "If only they knew" sets a predetermined level on how a person can interact with you. It's toxic and it can hurt relationships because we tend to respond in really unhelpful ways.

Whether we mean to or not, we will push people away when they are trying to care for us. We can become passive, embarrassed or downright avoid them at all costs. We may become resentful and manipulative to force someone to stay at a distance so that we can "prove" that we don't need their support. Why? Because we infer help as weakness in a society that prizes strength in independence above all things. This mentality and our ensuing actions block us from what we all desperately need: love and compassion. When we can begin to give ourselves grace, it opens up a realm where we can acknowledge that we don't have it all figured out and we actually need help. Realizing that we are not independent creatures designed to pick ourselves up by our boot straps is a gift that we can enjoy once we grasp the reality that we cannot do anything in this life alone.

If you are struggling with this from an emotional standpoint, let me speak pragmatically, from a physical standpoint. Even at the most trivial level we own clothing and eat meals and use cellphones or drive cars that come from the efforts of people *all over the world*. People who mine products, people who ship products, people who manufacture and distribute products, people who stand in a checkout line for hours on end to sell us products and then people who come every week to pick up our trash and recycling so that our homes do not turn into landfills. I don't know about you, but I did not make my toothbrush – someone else did. What a wonderful thing because I'd have terrible breath otherwise.

Now if you can extrapolate that physical reality to our jobs, businesses, opportunities, friends, books, groups, therapists, etc., you'll find that the sheer magnitude of our interconnectedness is astounding. I mean, even if you can't have empathy over a rough childhood or a difficult parenting situation, there is a leveling truth that our very existence in this life is due to the actions of others. It continues to open up that new dimension where we can see our interconnectedness far beyond the idiosyncrasies of our individual lives and into a vast and complex web of life. What does all of that mean for us?

We cannot do anything in this life alone.

Here's one of the shortest and most effective exercises you might ever come across. It might seem to you, at first, that it is as ridiculous as standing in front of a mirror and loving yourself. Once you test it out, however, and practice and really believe in it, it might change your life forever. So take a deep breath, calm your mind, and read this next sentence out loud:

I need help.

Pause. Sit with this for a moment. When is the last time you admitted that out loud? Does saying those words make you feel strong or weak? Part of this outreach for help means that we actually have to allow others to have grace on us. Allowing others to have grace on us is a further act of vulnerability and humility because you have to *let your guard down*. This is by no means an effortless feat. It takes immense courage and self-trust. Moreover, we are rarely taught the importance of this practice (I never found any college classes titled Trust 101 either).

Whether it is an act of compassion or forgiveness, it takes <u>strength</u> to admit we've made mistakes or we need help in the first place. If culture teaches us that needing help is defined as weakness, then why does it take so much more strength to admit you can't do it alone? Even for those of you who are hard-headed and stubborn like me, haven't you realized the more you try to do it alone, the harder the journey becomes, the more stress and fear will take hold, and ultimately, the chances of failure, disaster, or isolation will dramatically increase? Why do we avoid saying those three simple, miniscule, powerful words?

To understand exactly why, let's break this all down per the societal equation. It goes a little something like this:

needing help = vulnerability

vulnerability = weakness

weakness = failure

therefore, avoid needing help at all costs = **success**!

Awesome! Now we are all self-sufficient and miserable trudging through the seemingly endless difficulties of this world while simultaneously showing off our battle scars and professing everything is A-OK to keep our dignities and egos intact. All the meanwhile we miss a few key details; none of that stubbornness brings more vitality or love or grace into this world, none of it helps our relationships thrive, and none of it allows our communities to move forward in the depths of interconnectedness we are all intricately a part of.

So let's try something different.

Instead of pulling away, step forward. Let some-one hug you, forgive you, think about you, pray for you, help you or care for you. Take time to admit to yourself and to others the factual truth; we don't do anything in this world alone and we shouldn't have to think that we must. Find the courage and strength to receive grace as a gift. Only then can you become a part of the change to share that grace with others in turn. If I'm being truth-ful, I need that grace from you in this moment right now. Nothing about this book or my work is by any means per-fect. I have so much to learn and grow from. But we must not use that as an excuse to stop. We must not use that as an excuse to say, "it is the way it is" or "good enough."

This is a journey and we are all learning; let's keep learning together. So, if you ever get the chance to stand up and be vulnerable in front of a group or even just one friend, who cares if you forget the words or embarrass yourself. I couldn't be more grateful that I took a chance to share my story in front of a group – it was such a tiny step, and yet it forever changed the course of my life. Had I not taken that opportunity, these pages and this conversation, none of it would be before your eyes.

What a gift to share this small part of my journey with you.

CHAPTER 3 NOTES AND REFLECTIONS

How do you ask for help? What do you need to ask for help with? What small steps can you take to allow others into your life and your struggles? What does vulnerability look like for you? Remember this one small piece of extra homework: practice once a day saying "I need help" out loud. It will desensitize and destigmatize those three words allowing this work to happen more naturally.

_____

_____

_____

_____

_____

_____

_____

_____

_____

4

GIVING GRACE:

finding the gift in selflessness

"I'm not whole if you're not whole."
– Andy Soper

S ometimes I am exhausted by the idea of grace. It isn't natural to my upbringing, the societal influences in my life, or my culture. Therefore, it falls into the "change" category. That means I must engage, try, fail, try some more and hope that in time, grace becomes a subconscious habit. My life experiences have taught me to stay safe in my bubble. Change is too difficult so God created ice cream and Netflix as an alternative. Entertaining, but certainly not fulfilling long term. I'll be the first to admit it; grace can be really hard. As a matter of fact, I often find that giving grace is a lot more complicated than people expect. There is an ease in forgiving others or having compassion when things in your life are going relatively smoothly, but what about when they are not? When I'm having a bad day, when my world feels upside down, when I'm frustrated, tired, or "hangry," sometimes the last thing I want to do is give someone else grace – particularly if that grace involves my story.

How often do you find yourself consoling a friend in a café as they unpack their woes? Bestowing grace is important when a friend is mulling over a mistake or an issue in life and they need to hear a word of hope from someone they trust. But how often are you patiently sitting in that same café with a person who just turned your world upside down? When that hipster, wooden, yard sale chair you once thought was cute all of a sudden becomes the most uncomfortable chair in the world as you count the minutes until the conversation is over. Giving grace takes on a whole new meaning when this person and their mistakes have inflicted pain, frustration or discomfort on you. Let's be honest, we aren't usually sitting at that table.

Here is the real kicker though. Grace is not only important – it is *imperative* when it involves you personally. Case in point? Mary Johnson.

Mary was a single mother doing her best to raise her son Laramiun with all the difficulties life hurled her way. Over an argument at a party, twenty-year-old Laramiun was murdered by sixteen-year-old Oshea, a young man involved with gangs and drugs. At the end of his trial, Oshea was sentenced to twenty-five years in prison. Mary spoke about the hatred and anger she held for Oshea and all that she lost with her son's death. She would never see him graduate college, start a life of his own, marry and have children.

She spoke about the years she spent in darkness with her grief and her struggles to pray for and forgive her son's killer. After a decade of nursing those wounds, she began teaching a class at her church about forgiveness and had an epiphany asking herself: "How can I teach a class on forgiveness when I'm not even embodying the message myself?". Mary traveled to the prison to confront the man who took her son's life. By the end of the visitation, she found herself weeping in his arms and bestowing her forgiveness.

Impossible.

Most days I can't comprehend her journey through the pain and despair and I can't even begin to fathom the courage it must have taken for Mary to set foot in that prison. Yet when Oshea was released, he did not come home to an empty apartment but to a surprise "welcome home" party hosted by none other than Mary herself. A party filled with Mary and her son's friends who also wanted to welcome Oshea home to a new life with new opportunities to enable him to begin again.

Impossible.

Can you imagine? But as if that wasn't a great enough lesson in grace, the story doesn't end there. Today, Oshea lives next door to Mary and they travel the country speaking on the power of forgiveness, together.

"Unforgiveness is like cancer. It will eat you from the inside out," Mary advises.

Giving grace to others can take extraordinary strength, but the basis of forgiveness is not just in the reconciliation of the other. **It is about letting go of the toxins within you**. When you hold on to the bitterness and the resentment inside your heart, it will eat away at the foundation of your joy like acid on concrete. Consciously or subconsciously, it will detract from your ability to be fully present and experience all that life has to offer, here, in this moment. Even if the person did not harm you personally, it can be equally toxic to hold on to your judgments of them. Judgments and resentments hold weight and our brains are wired toward negativity. Neuroscientist and psychologist, Dr. Rick Hanson, relates negativity in the brain to Velcro and positivity to Teflon. In short, our brain is hardwired to protect us from harm in the natural world so it is always looking out for it. It's why we can receive ten positive compliments or emails and we will spend all of our time focusing on the one negative thing that person said about us. While I'm certainly not a neuroscientist, the overwhelming research in this department is hard to refute. Even if we remove emotion and look at this purely from a scientific point of view, it still speaks to the trite ways in which negativity consumes us and keeps us from progressing forward with our lives and our relationships.

Grace, on the other hand, taps into two things that hardly exist (or are given much weight) in most of our culture: *communication and compromise*. Have you ever felt like life is just a series of endless battles you must overcome to no avail? Oddly enough, we tend to communicate in that exact way. When someone hurts us, our typical response is not going to involve sitting calmly down at that café and asking questions or listening to that person to try and understand what he or she did, why they did it, and what they were hoping the outcome to be. That would be counterintuitive to the negativity bias in our brains. Instead, we forget the concept that hurt people hurt people and revert to a series of unhealthy responses. We become defensive, we attack, we hide, we avoid, we shame and guilt, we become passive aggressive, we gossip, we scheme, we plot, and most simply put, we find some way, shape or form to seek revenge.

It is no wonder how everything in life can feel like a string of battles. Grace has no place at the table when adrenaline is high and we are amped up for warfare because we never take the time to walk away, sit patiently, reflect or ask if this is something worth fighting about in the first place. Communication can be arduous since it is a two-way street. Even if we are strong, even if we approach things calmly full of I-statements like, "I feel hurt when you say _____," it is only half the equation. Say we are respectful, we don't lose our cool and we speak our mind in a healthy manner – we still have to hear the other person's point of view. It's often frustrating, but always important.

This leads us to the next order of business. We aren't always right. In fact, we are hardly ever *fully* right. We either directly or indirectly fail to communicate and we have something (small or large) to contribute to the story. What does that mean? On some level we have to compromise. The world isn't perfect, we don't always get what we want and we cannot control every aspect of every situation (even when we think we know what is best). That person has a completely different set of life experiences, circumstances, values and beliefs that are unique to them and we have to respect those in order to cultivate healthy relationships that flourish. Truthfully, this fact should bring a sigh of relief because it relinquishes us from the weight of always having to be right, to have the answers, and to know the "correct way." The power of grace alleviates some of the weight from our own shoulders, but it takes even more grace to share that reality with someone else.

This is where true forgiveness begins.

We often long for people to say they are "sorry" to us for the wrongs they have committed against us. I don't think that it is necessarily a bad thing to seek redemption and reconciliation (if it is possible). But how often are we looking for ways to intentionally say "I'm sorry" to someone else, like someone we may have hurt or caused distress? Let me put it very plainly. You make mistakes, yes? When you make those mistakes, how often do you earnestly wish that the other person will forgive you?

To let you off the hook, to give you a second or third or fourth chance to show them you can do better or be different or it won't happen again (even though it may)? I conveniently tend to forget this every time someone is hurting me.

To be clear, this is not a replacement for consequences. When Oshea committed a crime, he paid for it. And while our brains have been trained and wired toward negativity, Mary teaches us that the inability to bestow grace is another roadblock to experiencing greater joy in our lives. To change the story line, to take the time to rewire our brains toward grace leads us to a greater fulfillment of peace. The more in tune we are with this belief, the more love and compassion ultimately rules the day. This is not the "easy path" or else everyone would be doing it. This is the opportunity to look around at all of the pain in the world and say, "ENOUGH ALREADY"! It is time we try something different. Something toward the greater fulfillment and reconciliation in joy, not judgment, resentment and hate. The result is entirely dependent on the bar you set for what love and grace looks like in your community.

This is why compassion starts with giving yourself grace first, then receiving it, then followed by sharing it with others. Your perception of what grace means directly impacts all of your relationships and how you engage with the world. Grace and compassion, like communication and compromise, are two-way streets. Does it often feel like a one-way street? Absolutely. Nonetheless, someone has to start and unfortunately you have no control over how the other person responds. However, that is not the point. You cannot engage something out of guilt, shame or expectations. It will only bring frustration and resentment into your life and the relationships you are trying to foster. You have to enter into the conversation knowing that somewhere along the way, someone has shown grace and compassion on you, you know what that feels like and you long for more. But we cannot always receive more grace without the hard work of giving it away ourselves... *without* expectations of getting it back.

We have all faced and are currently facing battles in our lives that feel like endless cycles. Grace is the only way to not only disrupt those cycles but to break them altogether. That isn't effortless and can take enormous determination to accomplish. Sometimes that means tirelessly trudging through deep snow in the middle of a blizzard, but if you continue to be a voice of grace and compassion to those who need it most, including yourself, grace will ultimately win.

The other day I found myself sitting around a table leading a group of strangers through a 16-week men's collective class on formation. We gathered to discuss difficult, pressing issues in our communities and in our personal lives to try and invoke change in light of everything going on in the world. On the agenda that night, we were asked to write our eulogy. It was a sobering idea to tackle – what would I want people to remember me by? What kind of legacy would I want to leave behind for my daughter? Would I rather be known as a person full of love? Or to quote the great 1970's Foreigner hit, "You're as Cold as Ice"? Of course I want the first! To attain it, that starts with acknowledging the belief that, "I'm not whole if you're not whole." It gave me pause to reflect on a quote that stops me in my tracks every time I read it:

Whole people see and create wholeness wherever they go; split people see and create splits in everything and everybody.

– Richard Rohr

When we can engage the faults and follies of others and even the vices they hold against us, we can create a new conversation. By simultaneously receiving grace and having grace on ourselves, we can engage the opportunity to offer others grace. When we begin to offer grace back into the world, we take steps to make ourselves, and those around us, whole. We can begin to break the cycle of pain and despair in this world by acknowledging and seeing the brokenness and poorness we all share. By participating in that conversation, we change the dynamics of our relationships which trickles out into our communities. Or as Rohr said it best, we can see and create wholeness wherever we go.

That is a radical transformation.

That is a radical way of living.

That is a life worth striving for.

CHAPTER 4 NOTES AND REFLECTIONS

Where does your ability to offer grace end? What is your "impossible"? How can you engage those who have hurt you to hear about the pain that led them to hurt you in the first place? Write out a list of the people you need to offer grace to, why, and how you might take a small step toward doing so.

_____

_____

_____

_____

_____

_____

_____

_____

_____

_____

5

FINDING COMPASSION IN A BROKEN WORLD:

drama sells, starving kids doesn't

*"Darkness cannot drive out darkness; only light can do
that. Hate cannot drive out hate; only love can do that."*
– Martin Luther King Jr.

I remember the first time I heard the beatitude,
"Blessed are the poor, for theirs is the kingdom of
God" (Luke 6:20). I thought it sounded nice but was
also a rather cruel joke because there is no shortage of
suffering in this world caused by poverty. According to
the World Bank, almost half of the world's population
lives on less than $2.50 per day and nearly 71% of people

live on less than $10 per day. How do you take that beatitude seriously when our Central Intelligence Agency estimated the unemployment rate of Zimbabwe is 95% and there is physically no opportunity to lift yourself out of poverty or offer some of the basic necessities of life to your family?

Remember, this isn't about just the financially poor. Even in the United States, one of the world's richest countries, the story still rings true. According to groups like the Organization of Economic Cooperation and Development or the United Nations, America ranks somewhere around 14th on the Global Happiness Index. Even if you can't buy into a happiness index, it is safe to say that the American culture has a fair amount of societal pressure and performance stress that says if you are not growing, building, or achieving, you are in fact, lazy, incompetent, or failing.

I've seen beautiful things in this world, so don't get me wrong, but the nonstop bombardment of news, social media, hate crimes, politics, divisiveness, wars, poverty, genocide, terrorism, lying, cheating, scandals, natural disasters, and you name it, is a never-ending concoction of anxiety and desolate hopelessness. Yet when I read the news, I choose to read this stuff. I feel ignorant if I don't stay on top of the news and depressed if I do.

But good things do happen – and they happen every single day! What if it was all we ever heard about? What if we were bombarded 24/7 with just good things happening in the world? I'm not talking about cute kitten videos on repeat (although maybe that is the solution to all of our problems). But what if the latest person trying to get attention for spewing a hateful message on national TV got ... no attention? And what if that person who has devoted their life to saving neglected animals and works two jobs to afford the food it takes to keep going was the one on the news? I wonder if society would be rallying behind the call to save an animal versus buying a gun to hide under the mattress?

Our culture is addicted to violence and drama because violence and drama sells. From watching the theatrics unfold on reality TV (because we need to keep up with the Kardashians), to watching football, to people becoming famous on YouTube by trying to see how they can get drunk and do something stupid, you see this bleak reality. Drama and violence thrive in shows trying to dramatically save lives (like *Grey's Anatomy*) to shows trying to desperately kill every character off (like *Game of Thrones*... I still miss you Ned Stark). We are obsessed with watching people buy beachfront mansions and spending thousands of dollars on wedding dresses all in the name of "love." Television, movies, news, magazines and social media all keep us hooked through two distinct methods.

The first is very direct. Why is it so easy to watch a show featuring a family filled with nonstop fighting, hatred and jealousy? *Because it makes us feel better about ourselves.* When we think our life is hard, or we are crazy, or we have messed up, it's a relief to see there are people much "worse" than we are. We will unpack that more in a bit. The second method is a tad more subconscious. Have you ever seen shows like *The Bachelorette*? Why do I wish Sarah was actually giving the last rose to me and not Steve or Marquis? Well, because then I would be the one going on the yacht through the Bahamas. I'm not good enough to be on that yacht because I don't have twelve-pack abs, fifty million dollars, or perfect hair. Well I did have a perfect hair day once, but that's beside the point... Marquis has perfect hair *every day*.

Those are the two key selling points. The entire concept behind marketing and advertising is to convinces you that you *need* something. You will be a better person, life will be easier, you will look better, you will be healthier, your friends and family will be envious, you will masterfully become complete all for the low, low price of $9.99. It doesn't matter if they're seeking to sell you cars, make up, cell phones, houses, vacations, outfits,

TV shows, or gym memberships; the point is that whatever you are, wherever you are and whoever you are right
now, is *not good enough*. If you don't have an 80" screen
TV, you cannot properly watch a hockey game. If you do
not own the new Corvette, something is wrong with your
manhood. If you cannot fit into a size three dress, you
are not taking the right pills. If you are stressed, there
is a prescription for that too. You cannot sit on a bus,
read a news article, or listen to music in peace. Heck, I
cannot even go to the bathroom now without "stall talk
advertisements." Seriously! Whoever thought that was a
good idea, let me go to the bathroom in peace! Research
estimates that we see as many 5,000 advertisements a
day. Let that sink in for a minute.

5,000 advertisements a day.

That means 5,000 times a day I am told I am not
good enough and I need something more. Then we come
home to sit and watch TV and never wonder why the
people who have it "all" are still so unhappy and their
families have as much baggage as our own. No wonder
our culture is so addicted to drama and violence – it distracts us from our "not enough-ness."

Here is the distressing truth in this scenario of
demoralizing culture shock. Having only eight minutes
to save the world from an alien explosion is sexy; it grasps

our attention and leaves our hearts racing as we cling to popcorn soaked in fake butter. Talking about starving kids in Yemen, well, it isn't very "sexy" at all. In fact, you could say that the alien movie distracted me from all the pain in this world; it's entertaining and it's probably got a happy ending. Why do you think the movie theater industry exploded during the Great Depression of the 1930s even though people could barely afford to feed their families? Talking about suffering, on the other hand, makes us feel guilty when we have luxury and choose not to help. It also makes us reflect on our own pain and poorness, which are the things we are trying to avoid by using entertainment in the first place.

So how does this apply to this moment now? While writing this book, I've noticed my news feed is filled with one form of negativity or another every day. I don't tend to like the presumptuous notions of comparisons, but to some degree, I believe there are issues we should be focused on more so than others. Our president can get into a Twitter fight with a celebrity and the whole country is in an uproar about who said what to whom. Yet twenty million people in sub Saharan Africa are currently facing famine and it is hardly discussed. What plausible excuse could we possibly have for such embarrassing behavior?

Many folks say we have to worry about problems of our own: "Not in my back yard, not my problem." Ok, fine. Tell me about what you are doing to make a difference in your "back yard." Most folks I meet don't have a strong answer for that. Moreover, where does your back yard begin and end? Your literal back yard? Your neighborhood? Your city? Your country? But wait a minute, aren't we all "one" anyway? Just once, perhaps, we can put down the razor-sharp edge of our #2 graphite pencils where we draw the distinct line of "who is in and who is out."

~~It's not working.~~

<u>It has never worked</u>.

Let's reverse this train of thought because I like to think the test for this is very simple. Skip or delay a meal long enough for your stomach to grumble and then ask yourself if you could do that for the rest of the day, or multiple days, or perhaps for months wondering where and when you would find your next meal. If you could feel the pain of hunger, would you want someone to share a meal with you if they could? Now take that one step further and picture yourself sitting on the doorstep of a person's house that has a bit of financial power, and they come outside looking up from their smartphone to make eye contact with you for just a moment. In this instance they can do one of two things; 1) go back to their phones or 2) reach out a hand. What if instead of sharing a meal that person chose to Tweet about how obscene someone's outfit was because that was more important than your survival? We treat people as though they are disposable, yet our cell phones aren't.

Now if this was about guilt and shaming, put me first in line because I can't tell you the last time I was "starrrrrving" and didn't use my cellphone to find the nearest restaurant. This is about a larger reflection of our societal brokenness – the brokenness of our world and cultural views. It is not about saying we aren't doing enough, it is about acknowledging that *we aren't doing anything at all.* There is a Bible verse that terrifies me to this day in which a young man asked Jesus what it was that he still lacked – after all, he was doing everything "right." Jesus responded with, "If you want to be perfect, go, sell all your possessions and give it to the poor, and you will have treasure in heaven. Then come, follow me." (Matthew 19:21). I have never met a Christian who took that seriously. Those are called saints and they are the ones history writes about. Yet I've watched many Christians claim they take the Bible seriously, word for word, who have never come near that verse. And if this paragraph makes your blood boil a bit, then good!

I don't say any of this to be rude, but to offer a pause for reflection in our own humility. It's a chance to stop pointing fingers elsewhere and see all the changes we can make within ourselves. It's an opportunity to ask honest questions like, "Am I doing the best I can with the resources and time that I have? Or do I serve based on what is convenient for my calendar and bank account?" I know I typically fall into the latter category. But I also believe this conversation is an opportunity to focus more on that humbling truth and less on what everyone else is doing. To focus on what is actually important in life and not on all the noise that distracts us from it. As my friend Ashton Gustafson says, "Our days need to be more and more about less and less."

One more note: this conversation is also not about capability. We are more than capable to serve and to help in all sorts of ways; I believe we are told we can't. Forgiveness, compassion and service; these things are hard work because we believe them to be. We have been taught that it is easier to belittle, to bully, to judge, to preserve ourselves and our bank accounts, to seek redemption in television shows rather than redemption in relationships or humility. We are taught to take the quick, easy escape of distractions and ignore the long-term adverse impacts that they have on our lives and relationships.

I won't deny it, we all have a #2 graphite pencil in our back pocket; we must have boundaries to keep some form of sanity in our lives otherwise we would burn out. Self-care is a critical component of being able to not only serve but to serve well. But I find it more common that we are burning out from political feuds with the in-laws, not from serving in our community. We need to be woken up from this self-indulging lifestyle to become the good news our communities so desperately need.

So where do we draw the line? And is it that simple?

I went to a church gathering at a farm a few years back where the founder of The Simple Way, Shane Claiborne, came to speak. There must have been three or four hundred people there with an endless buffet of fresh food. It was one of those flawless evenings with the setting sun casting an orange glow over the fields. Right before the scheduled speech, a hippie looking fellow came up to me and tried to spark up a conversation. He wore baggy homemade clothes and had a thick southern accent and long dreads; I was afraid I was about to get sucked into a discussion about legalizing marijuana again. I tried to break free so I could get a good seat to listen to the infamous author and revolutionary activist, Shane, speak. Dodging the conversations and sneaking to the third row I was eager to get a glimpse of the speaker I'd come to see.

Lo and behold, that baggy-clothed-dreaded-hair-hippie walked up on to the stage and introduced himself as Mr. Claiborne. I could only sigh to myself in embarrassment. I felt like a real donkey (and not the cute kind at the petting zoos). The first thing Shane did was hold up a newspaper with two cover articles; the first was about the obesity epidemic in America and the second article was about a famine in Africa. It made me squirm in my chair. He went on to speak about things he had learned over the years by working with folks like Mother Teresa. One thing stuck out that stings me to this day: "If you own two coats," he said, "it's because you've taken one from someone in need."

Yikes...

He said it was that simple. I squirmed in my chair that much more. Let me be transparent for a moment here. I owned more than two coats when he spoke those words. In fact, I still own more than two coats to this day. But the more I've grown in my own life, the more I can understand and comprehend the weight of that statement without some of the knee-jerk theatrics. Not because it's my job or philosophy to "save the world" anymore, but I've adopted a new, healthier perspective: if

I was cold, if I was hungry, or when I'm sad, when I'm hurting, would I want someone to share a coat or meal or an embrace with me? So much of my life has been on my terms. I liked donating money, when I had a salary. I loved volunteering, when it didn't inconvenience my schedule. Neither was hardly a sacrifice at all for me back then. Just like my coat closet, I had, (and in many ways still have) shallow viewpoints when it comes to acts of service even though I know I'm called to so much more in this life.

You may not agree with Shane's lifestyle, but you also can't deny the numbers. Shane's small community has raised and dispensed tens of millions of dollars to cover finances, pay for medical bills, rebuild homes and help with all of the obstacles that come from life to those who need help in their community. Money that was raised from the bank accounts of members within their community alongside an untold number of volunteer hours. This is why their philosophy is so simple; when you have abundance, you share – when you are in scarcity, you receive. Everyone is worthy to receive love, grace and compassion not only in their back yard, but around the world.

This community invites us to see an alternative to our "service of convenience" lifestyle. Just like the failing of convenient compassion, our service cannot be pre-determined on convenience. I'll repeat it until I'm blue in the face: this isn't about guilt and shame as that will not ultimately help the situation or engage us from an authentic place. This is about an invitation to enter into a new life with a higher altitude. We should not be afraid of challenging dialogue that pushes our comfort zone. That is our opportunity to learn new ways, to grow. It's a chance to connect with the stories of others as the best living examples that show us a new perspective and a better way to carry out a new narrative.

In *The Book of Joy*, by Douglas Abrams, Archbishop Desmund Tutu shared a story that I had to reread over and over again because I couldn't believe it. Amidst acts of genocide during the apartheid in South Africa, some young men went to a village of a different tribe and murdered several other young men. They dragged their bodies back through the town square to show off, boasting with pride, what they had done. At the trial for their murders, the punishment was swift. Jail and death. The mothers of the slain boys came to the trial to publicly forgive the boys who murdered their children in an attempt to say that no justice would come from putting these kids in jail or in the ground; it would not end the cycle.

Impossible.

Of course the story doesn't end there. As if that wasn't enough compassion, the mothers started a non-profit to raise money to give the young men jobs and become members of society again. Let that sink in for a minute. Would you start a non-profit for the person who killed your family member or child? Or would you do everything in your power to lock them up for life?

Beyond impossible.

Or is it that simple?

There is no use trying to imagine the pain and heartache those women went through and the strength and the courage it took to not only forgive, but then to serve the murderers of their children. They saw beyond their pain to recognize the brokenness of these young men. How much more love, grace and humility could you possibly show?

Three years ago I found myself at a conference for rebuilding a community. I remember watching a presentation on a compassion project where inmates at a female prison facility were given a rewards system based on acts of compassion, for an eleven-day trial study. In those eleven days there wasn't <u>a single reported case of violence in the entire prison</u>. They took the strategy to gang-ridden high schools that averaged dozens of incidents per day and concluded the same result.

Impossible.

Or is it that simple?

Is it not only possible, but highly plausible, that compassion doesn't just exist in a broken world – it has the ability to *thrive*. In fact, I'm going to argue that compassion is the only way moving forward.

What if we all tuned in to a different story line away from the negativity of our culture to create an abundance of good news? What if we all shared our extra coat and cooked a meal for a stranger and participated in the healing and redemption of communities around the world?

You have that kind of power,

right here,

in this moment,

now.

~~Impossible.~~

Simple.

CHAPTER 5 NOTES AND REFLECTIONS

What is keeping you from engaging compassion in your life? Where is your "back yard" located? Who is welcome and who is not? What steps could you take to extend that boundary? Who could you give a coat to, or share a meal with, or donate your time to?

_____

_____

_____

_____

_____

_____

_____

_____

_____

_____

_____

_____

6

WHAT IF HE OR SHE WAS GOD?

"When we hear people referred to as animals or aliens, we should immediately wonder, 'Is this an attempt to reduce someone's humanity so we can get away with hurting them or denying them basic human rights?'"
— Brené Brown

L iving in downtown Grand Rapids, as you would expect in any city of substantial size, there is a large homeless population. I once believed that I would finally be at peace in the world when I could look at a homeless person and feel utter compassion. If I'm going to be straightforward, I used to always feel bitter when someone would ask me for money and give me a story about needing to buy bus tickets. Growing up around substance abuse, I became resentful of the effects that drugs and alcohol had on people and of being lied to. It always stirred something deep and dark from my childhood which would make my blood boil.

At the same time, it was hard to see the pain and struggle and simultaneously feel comfortable lying when I said I had nothing to give. I logically recognized that giving money wasn't going to help. There is no shortage of food or resources in my community and I knew statistically where every dollar went from panhandling (from information given to me by the organizations serving the homeless). But I began to get more involved with local organizations to face my anger, to sit with folks on the street and hear their story and their side of things. I learned that giving money could actually be harmful... but there are so many ways to give beyond pocket change.

I learned more about mental illnesses and it tied back into my knowledge that people don't drink, or do drugs, or become homeless because everything has been perfect in their lives. There was a deep pain and isolation in the story of each person I met because they severed all remaining forms of support they had left. In fact, it resounded with the very same thing I found every person, homeless or not, was searching for – a sense of meaning, love, purpose and belonging in this world.

I had built my restaurant around a concept of offering free meals to those in need. I remember one day checking folks out at the counter and this family gave money to their two kids to purchase "taco tickets" to give to a homeless gentleman sitting at a table nearby. It was picture perfect, maybe even billboard perfect, like I cooked it up in a marketing lab somewhere. Those who had were not only sharing but teaching their children to share with those who didn't have anything. But I didn't want to leave the impression that only people struggling financially would get a free meal. We began giving out free meals to anybody I could think of in an effort to demonstrate that everyone has worth in our community. If I ask you to describe for me a person in "need," you will likely paint me a person of financial poverty. Yet as we discussed before, poverty comes in so many forms and we all have needs regardless of our wealth.

Grand Rapids is a medical hub in Western Michigan, so it was common to see many patrons visiting from hospital settings. On a Wednesday afternoon, one woman went into our overflow side room to eat lunch by herself. She was crying over her meal and I couldn't help but ask her what was wrong. She confided in me that her husband was in the middle of heart surgery and she didn't know what she would do without him. I pulled some tickets off the wall and let her know that someone had paid for her meal. One of my employees looked at me sternly, saying, "But she can afford her meal," to which I bluntly responded, "And so can I."

There is a beautiful story known as the "Rabbi's Gift" which I'll summarize as best I can, hopefully without damaging the integrity of the metaphor. A once great and flourishing monastery was down to four elderly monks and their leader, the abbot. Desperate to save their dying order, the abbot went to a local rabbi to ask for advice. After conversing for a while, the rabbi confessed to the abbot that he had no advice for him. Eager for anything the abbot pressed one more time. The rabbi stated that the only thing he knew was that the Messiah was one of them. Dumbfounded, the abbot returned to the monastery to share what he was told. The monks discussed amongst themselves the strengths and weakness of each person but no one could determine who the Messiah was within that monastery. So, the four remaining monks and abbot began to treat each other as though each one could, in theory, be *the* Messiah. Eventually

through the kindness and compassion they had for each
other, people began to take notice. They couldn't help
but wonder what was behind the enchanting mystery.
As folks trickled back in, the dying monastery grew and
thrived once more.

It doesn't really matter if you are a Christian, a
Buddhist, Muslim, spiritual or don't practice any form
of religion at all, the story fits. Whether you believe or
don't, let's all sit at the same table and say for a moment
that there could be a divine entity that is behind it all.
What if it were true that the person you're honking at
in traffic, the co-worker having a stressful day, the person sitting on the side of the road, the cashier at checkout, the bank teller, or even your spouse was indeed the
Messiah? How differently would you treat that person?
How easy would it be to forgive them for a mistake? Or
show more compassion and kindness toward them?

Imago Dei translates into "image of God" from the
Book of Genesis. It folds into this notion that you are
made in the image of God or made in the gift of divine
love. This phrase is where my heart longs to be. To know
the very essence of everyone's soul is rooted in abounding love. I have these moments when I can see past my
own frustrations, ulterior motives, and judgments to see
anyone, including myself, glowing in the gift of divine

love. It transforms my way of engaging with a person from "are they doing the best that they can?" into "they are doing the best that they can with what they know to be true." It takes away this notion of who is right and wrong, who is trying the hardest, who knows what is best, and evolves my interactions into giving everyone the benefit of the doubt.

My back yard expands to include... *everyone*.

This isn't necessarily easy and I'm lucky to stay on this track for long, but it can even take weight off of myself and my burdens for what I believe to be true or best for my community. It allows a bit of grace and compassion to enter into the space between relationships to acknowledge that it is unlikely either of us has it "figured out," but that we are instead all learning in this life together. The more I believe that anyone and everyone is made in the image of God, the more fruitful my interactions become.

The first time I heard some friends talk about "energy," I thought they were crazy. Then after graduating with a degree in Natural Resource Management, I realized everything in life is dependent upon the flow of energy. It's how plants photosynthesize to grow, how waves move, how a tree dies and becomes soil again. It's the same for us humans. We depend upon eating food to get energy for all bodily functions and survival. Our brain controls our muscles through electrical impulses. Our very heart beats due to this framework of electric currents of energy. In fact, depending on what scientist you talk to, we have about 10 billion neurons firing every single second of our living existence. That's a lot of energy! Have you ever walked into a room and just *felt* the tension? Have you ever been *lost* staring into someone's eyes or at the slightest touch of a lover's hand? What causes these things to happen? You can't give me a scientific explanation on where feelings come from, but we all know they exist. We are communicating all the time without so much as speaking a word.

What I would like to argue here is the science behind 70% of communication being non-verbal is much more significant than we acknowledge. But it's how we engage with that 70% that matters. When we recognize someone with the notion that they may be a child of the divine or that they are made in the image of divine love, our posture toward that person changes. The tone in which we speak to them and the way we look at or interact with them changes. The way we shift our energy changes. It is seen, it is heard, it is *felt*. This dialogue is so much larger than just the words we speak. And the more we see and feel the respect and dignity of being treated with such kindness and compassion, the more likely we are to pass it along to others. The more we offer that to others, the larger the domino effect becomes, and the more that dying monastery begins to flourish with love once more.

It is not a perfect equation. Someone will start the pay-it-forward line at Starbucks and someone having a bad day will break that chain. We all have our bad days, we all have our off moments. That is when we need the gift of divine love from others the most. It is easier to love someone when they are kind, when you are having a good day, when the sun is shining and everything just seems to be going your way. It is much, much harder to love a stranger asking you for money when you're trying to find a job. To love your friend when you found out that they just lied to you. To love your kid when they just told you that you're the worst parent in the world. To love your boss when they say you did a terrible job. To love that person spewing retched hate and violence in the world... to actually, tangibly love your enemies.

I get it; we don't live in a perfect world. There is no acoustic guitar and Kumbaya circle on every street corner. Life is hard. In fact, life can be downright ridiculously difficult at times. But sometimes, in the midst of our pain, anger, fears, frustrations, jealousy, resentments and judgments, this spark of hope comes into sight. We realize how badly we want people to love and forgive us through our countless mistakes. We acknowledge that we don't know the other person's whole story and ultimately, we give them the benefit of the doubt. We choose to offer them love instead – even when we might not want to, and we are not expecting it in return, we know it's the only path forward if we desire to ever receive it ourselves.

We must confess that we don't know all of the answers. It's actually very hard to make sense of galaxies and planets, and trees and energy and life and the ability to feel. Yet we are always invited to partake in a greater awareness. One that we cannot sum up in words or in a book no matter how hard we try. Once we realize there is a possibility that we are sons and daughters of the divine, whatever the divine means for you, then we leave room for the possibility that each person we encounter is made in the image of God, a gift of divine love.

CHAPTER 6 NOTES AND REFLECTIONS

How do you get more connected with the "energy" in your life? What does your monastery look like? What does Imago Dei mean for you and your relationships? What "enemies" of yours need your grace?

_____

_____

_____

_____

_____

_____

_____

_____

_____

_____

_____

_____

PART 2

THE ROADMAP TO HOLISTIC COMPASSION

"You say you care about the poor?
Tell me, what are their names?"
—*Gustavo Gutierrez*

7

COMPASSION WILL COST YOU SOMETHING:

that shouldn't be a bad thing

"More than any other single way the grace of humility is worked into our lives through the discipline of service... Nothing disciplines the inordinate desires of the flesh like service, and nothing transforms the desires of the flesh like serving in hiddenness. The flesh whines against service but screams against hidden service. It strains and pulls for honor and recognition."
– Richard Foster

The truth is that none of this is easy. All things worth doing take time and that alone isn't easy when most of us struggle with patience.

Compassion takes empathy and it takes vulnerability. It takes letting go of your pride and letting go of your ego. It takes humility. Most of all, *compassion takes time.*

Best of all, perhaps, is this: compassion is a skill, not an inherent trait. It is something you must learn and practice, attain and fine tune. It's not something you're either born with or you're not; it can always be cultivated to a greater extent. It will take years – a lifetime – to master. Even then, there is always more to learn and further to go. Compassion is a journey without an endpoint.

In today's world, remember we are constantly bombarded with messages grasping for our attention. It was in my lifetime that people still read books in school to learn what the book was about. There was no easy-access to "SparkNotes." You couldn't turn to Google in a gadget in your pocket to look up a quick synopsis of *The Old Man and the Sea* right before class. If you wanted to pass the test, you actually had to do the work and read the book.

With the internet came the dawn of YouTube where you had to watch two and half minutes of rambling in order to get to the funny part of a young man stepping off the edge of a 30-foot tree swing screaming an ear-piercing, high-pitched squeal (it sounded like I was at a Backstreet Boys concert with a group of teenage girls).

Now, we have trimmed everything down to five second Snapchats and 280-character Tweets. Advertisers have even figured out that their ads need to be less than 30 seconds or they will lose the viewer. The mantra has become: don't make me read, don't make me watch, don't make me think. Give it to me with as little detail in as short amount of time as possible. And we wonder why our political system is broken (or any system for that matter)? We are all competing for non-stop 30 second waves in a battle of attention.

Compassion is not something you can cram into a Facebook status update or a text message. It is a way of living. Can an act of compassion take 30 seconds? Without a doubt, it can. Sometimes it can be as simple as asking the person who is taking your lunch order how their day is going. But it's more than listening to a speaker about the trials of a disease and donating a few dollars on their website. It's more than giving a hug at a funeral and uttering the words "I'm sorry for your loss." If we long for a better world, if we long for a life filled with meaning and purpose, if we long for restitution and justice, if we long for joy and love and belonging, then compassion is going to cost us something.

More often than not, I am incredibly fortunate to meet many wonderful souls in my line of work. In the chaos of today's world, it is such a gift to be able to reflect with another person on issues that actually matter in this life, matters beyond the hustle and bustle of our success-driven culture. Sometimes, I meet people who just stop me in my tracks. They inspire and move me in ways I can't always describe.

Leslie King is one of those people. I remember the first time I got to sit and have coffee with Leslie. It was an afternoon of fancy artisanal coffee, locally baked goods and the deep intimacy of conversation that occurs when sharing authentic vulnerability with a stranger. By the end of our discussions I said to her, "I already feel like you are another mom to me." She chuckled and replied, "Everyone calls me Momma Leslie." Leslie was coerced into the streets at the age of 15. Forced into sex slavery, she turned her first trick (sexually exploited) before she was legally allowed to drive. Drugs and alcohol followed; for two decades, Leslie would call the streets her home. After attempting suicide, she encountered what she could only describe as God, found the courage to walk away from her life on the streets and began a new path for herself. Her non-profit, Sacred Beginnings, began in 2005 and is dedicated to rescuing victims and facilitating long-term healing of sex-enslaved and trafficked women. "As a prostitute you are labeled before you walk through the door," she explained. "I know the pain all too well... I know them even if they don't know themselves."

You don't have to face sex slavery or drug abuse to be cared for and loved by Leslie. And you only have to know her for all of five minutes. For Leslie, it is simple. She can see the pain we are all bearing and will sit with you to meet you where you are at because she knows the importance of connection; of feeling loved unconditionally without judgment.

None of us have to face extreme traumas to know this to be true – to know the gift of being loved and being loved well. Remember our brief discussion about the surface level attachments our brain has toward negativity? Well let's take it a step deeper past that into the higher reasoning of our brain and who we are. Yes, our mammalian brains are hardwired toward negativity, but we are also hardwired for connection... literally. Amy Banks is the author of multiple books, a medical doctor, the director of advanced training at the Jean Baker Miller Institute and a Harvard professor (just to highlight a few items on her resume). Amy was asked in an interview what she meant in saying that humans are "hardwired to connect," and she responded:

Neuroscience is confirming that our nervous systems want us to connect with other human beings. A good example of this is mirror neurons, which are located throughout the brain and help us read other people's feelings and actions. They may be the neurological underpinnings of empathy – when two people are in conversation they are stimulating each other's mirror neuron system. Not only will this lead to movement in similar muscles of the face (so the expressions are similar) but it also allows each [person] to feel what the other is feeling. This is an automatic, moment to moment resonance that connects us. There have been studies that look at emotions in human beings such as disgust, shame, and happiness, where the exact same areas of the brain light up in the listener who is reading the feelings of the person talking. We are, literally, hardwired to connect.

Impressive, right? I feel smarter just from reading that. But I want to take us past the science back to Chapter Three when we began discussing this idea of interconnectedness. There is nothing in this life you can do alone. Personally, I always prided myself on the capability to do everything by myself in order to evade being perceived as weak or vulnerable in asking for help. Yet whether your goal is becoming a recluse from the world or trying to stand on top of it, you don't do either alone. Rooting ourselves in this humility should be a daily ritual.

Our interconnectedness goes beyond acknowledging that we need help. To ground ourselves once more I find it pertinent to be reminded of some basic principles; you didn't pave the roads you travel on, or build the television you watch, or harvest the trees that built your shelter. If you drink water, or eat food, or wear clothes (and I hope you do all three), someone had a hand in making your life easier, making your life more comfortable so you can enjoy the things you really want to enjoy. Even if you try to be as humanly independent as possible, it is physically impossible that your life wasn't improved or made possible by the interactions of others. No matter how hard or inconvenient this truth may be, the fact remains that your physical presence is a gift from others. We are deeply connected beings.

When we can grasp just how connected we are, it makes it easier to tap into our deep sources of compassion. You are needed, you matter, you are worthy and you play a role in this life, in this world. You have a purpose. As hard as it is to see sometimes, that person who hurt you, that person whom you don't know, and that person on the other side of the world you will never so much as see in a picture, has a purpose.

We all have a purpose.

Getting lost in our negative emotions robs us of our ability to see this, remember this, or acknowledge it in ourselves or in those around us. I go back and forth on whether or not it is easier to be angry and judge or if it is easier to forgive and have grace. Initially, of course anger and judgments are always easier. Taking the time to process, to have patience, or to contemplate the struggles of another can be emotionally and even physically taxing. But in the long run, I believe full heartedly that subtle frustration or resentment will consume you. It will consume infinitely more life and energy and mental space than it would take in the initial stages to be present with that person in the first place. Karen Armstrong said in her book, *Twelve Steps to a Compassionate Life:*

> We don't want to listen to the sad story that a colleague is telling us. We feel that we have enough to deal with and push her troubles from our mind. We can be irritated by somebody's bad mood instead of asking ourselves why she is depressed... Remember the things that help you when you are having a bad day – a kind word, a smile, a joke – and try to give that gift to a testy colleague. Remember what it is like to feel alone with sadness and take the trouble to listen to your friend's tale of woe.

Compassion will cost you something because it means investing, not only your time and energy to engage the struggles of another, but it also means letting go of your own outcomes and expectations of the results. We live in a "fix it" culture. I mean, in a pinch, there is always duct tape, right? We want it to be a quick and painless fix, but we also want it to work properly – how we see fit. We tend to know what the person did wrong and what they need to do in order to resolve the issues at hand. In the process of our all-knowing-knowledge, we negate some simple truths. Like for instance, we don't actually know what we are talking about. I know, I know, but you are the all-wise-being on the other end of these pages. Stay with me...

Even if we know what we are talking about, it is really hard to realize that we actually don't. You woke up today, ate a meal, perhaps went to work or took a shower, all individual moments of time. A million, billion, gazillion things (very scientific, I know) have taken place in the context of history that have led to this precise moment that allowed you to exist and do the very things you are doing in this moment. My ancestors immigrated to this country, made some good decisions and some poor decisions in their lives, someone decided to build a town here, and survived through famine and diseases and world wars. Infinite decisions and possibilities had to take place for generations before my parents would meet and I would be conceived (did I mention I was a "whoopsie" baby). Someone decided to put in water and sewer pipes so I could shower, someone decided to build the mattress that I sleep on, and someone decided to make a living to grow the food that I would eat.

Your life in and of itself is an intricate, complex web of infinite possibilities and decisions that come together to make the moment in which you are reading this very paragraph possible. Is it conceivable then, in the simplest of situations, that the person you are engaging with had a complex array of moments and experiences that led up to this instance? Is it possible that even with the best of intentions you do not know the complexities (in their entirety) of what tomorrow will bring? That you don't know the exact outcome, with 100% certainty, that choosing option A over B would entail?

Are there choices to make that might lean toward more favorable outcomes? Absolutely. But in our desire to know all and to control all, we bear the weight of the world and those complexities that are far beyond our reasoning and control. So, it should be a relief, not a cause for fear, that we do not know every detail of a person's situation and we don't have control over what happens next in their life. Furthermore, there is no shame or judgment or resentment you can share with that person that they aren't likely already feeling themselves. So what good is it to stroke your ego and rub salt in a wound? Instead, we can embrace that we can do our best to walk in their shoes, to feel their pain, and to be present knowing that they may be trying as best as they can to live and survive in all the intricacies and complexities this life has to offer.

Having compassion means letting go of the outcome in the situation. Do we want that person to apologize, to make amends, to right their wrongs? No doubt we do, but life is not a balancing scale of a perfect justice system and trying to keep score is downright exhausting. The only way to move forward is to let go of your desires and free yourself from that burden. As an alternative, offer someone else what you so desperately seek yourself – love, grace and forgiveness. This trio lies at the heart of what makes compassion possible.

I can't fathom the strength it took those mothers in South Africa to do what they did, or what Mary did to change the course of Oshea's life forever, or the courage it takes Leslie to return to the streets that took twenty years of her life, but that kind of compassion these people share is available for us all. That is the level of compassion that we can reach in order to make this world a better place.

It's time to take all of these discussions and align them toward concrete actions to integrate compassion as a habit into our lives. AJ Sherrill breaks compassion down into a roadmap with four intersections: sympathy, empathy, solidarity and generosity. We oftentimes want to skip right from sympathy into generosity, but for tangible change to occur, we *must* experience and engage all four intersections. It takes humility. It takes letting go of our pride, egos, agendas and expectations. And it also takes time. This journey is going to cost you something, but without a shadow of a doubt, I believe the reward is worth so much more. Let's take the first step when we open our posture to listen to the cry of another.

The roadmap to holistic compassion:

CHAPTER 7 NOTES AND REFLECTIONS

Do you need people to acknowledge your acts of kindness? What steps could you take to move toward unconditional kindness or "hidden service"? What ways do you engage your relationships in life from a "fix it" point of view? How could you engage those relationships with more presence while letting go of the outcomes and expectations?

_____

_____

_____

_____

_____

_____

_____

_____

_____

_____

8

SYMPATHY:

I hear your cry

. . . .

*"Our blessing comes not in separation from the poor,
but in identification with them." – AJ Sherrill*

. . . .

There is a beautiful quote by Thich Nhat Hanh: "Understanding someone's suffering is the best gift you can give to another person. Understanding is love's other name. If you don't understand, you can't love." He speaks about how love is expansive like a tree – the moment it stops growing, it begins to die. Compassion, like love, must continually grow or it will begin to die. Why? Because if we aren't giving it to others, it is a reflection that we aren't giving it to ourselves. If we aren't giving it to ourselves, then we are slowly caving in on ourselves.

We have to understand the profound impact that compassion has on those around us, but we cannot help another person's suffering if we do not understand it. To understand someone's suffering we must first sit and listen. The basic act of sitting still and listening is so crucial but is so commonly overlooked. It is where sympathy starts, but it takes time because pain is not something that can be summed up in one conversation. Often, a moment of devastation can stem from a series of events spanning a longer period of time, even if the moment of impact seems so singular. I want to make sure we get this first step into context otherwise our next three steps are null and void.

I spent many of my childhood summers visiting North Carolina where my dad's side of the family lived. The highlights, without question, revolved around my cousin Janice. The family called her "Tootsie," but to this day, I could not tell you why. Tootsie's kitchen was always filled with the smell of freshly baked homemade biscuits and sweet tea. It was a half mile walk from my father's front porch down the dusty, country backroad to the side door that led right into her kitchen. Sometimes the walk felt never ending, but the chorus of birds and insects always kept me company and I can't tell you a single morning I visited when breakfast wasn't already waiting for me on the table, whether my visit was planned or not.

I remember Tootsie's horses, the countless dogs she rescued, Speedy the goat who always wanted to play, and her endless collection of salt and pepper shakers. I bought her unique ones at every yard sale I went to including my favorite; a bear hugging a beehive. I remember the good days filled with laughter in her ever-so-unique crackling laugh sitting on her favorite swing with friends gathered round. I remember the not-so-good days filled with pain, sorrow and hardship as she would sniffle away her tears to hide it. And I remember the day when her cancer came out of remission. It seemed routine, chemo-therapy treatments every Thursday morning; she was a tough cookie. And then she missed treatment one week and had to wait until the following week to receive treat-ment again. It was all downhill from there as the cancer abruptly took a turn.

Even as a kid I could sense things were not going according to plan. The subtle nuances added up as the months progressed. I began to take notice because the horses were gone. The many dogs became the few. Then the few disappeared. The chickens were gone, Speedy was nowhere to be found and the remaining hay in the

barn lay stagnant. Her half-acre garden where I'd harvest more beans and squash and watermelon than I
knew what to do with was overgrown with weeds. I saw
Tootsie's pain, I heard her words of despair and felt her
tears. I visited her for the last time when she was lying in
a hospital bed that hospice had brought to her home so
she could die in the place she loved most.

Tootsie was the centerpiece of my dad's family. Most
families have one, that person who is the glue holding
everyone together by calming the family quarrels and
gathering everyone for the holidays. She wasn't perfect,
but she was deeply loved by most. To some, her death
seemed like it was just another funeral for a person
whose time had come. For my dad's side of the family, it
would be the end of all family reunions and what good
times came from my visits to North Carolina.

We tend to look at things as singular moments of
impact. A death, a job loss, a divorce – each seen as an
isolated incident. But there tends to be so much weight
behind them all, so many intricate pieces to the story
that led up to these "big" moments of life. There just isn't
any time to deal with those big moments let alone all of
the time it would take to invest in the smaller moments
that lead up to them. People don't typically wake up on
a Tuesday and say it's a good day to leave their spouse.

There is so many moments of connection and experiences and friends and families and decisions that lead up to the big moment. But we usually fail to see this; we have become an overly connected society without any real connection. It is a quiet devastation that is consuming the very fabric that holds us all together. It leaves no room for remorse, no room for proper grieving, and no room to understand another's suffering.

I'll put this in a better frame of reference. Tootsie wasn't just losing her life, there were great consequences to her sickness and death. There were animals that no longer received her love. Her husband was illiterate and she ran the books for the family business. She was the tender heart that people spilled their sorrows to. You can buy biscuits at the store, but they won't ever be Tootsie's biscuits. It's complicated. It's bigger than we give it time for.

To be present with someone's suffering requires listening beyond the moment of impact. To have sympathy, to hear someone's cry, you need to be present for all of it. Somewhere along the way, we determine it is too much for our overloaded schedules.

Chuck DeGroat, with support from research by Brigid Schulte, breaks down our busyness in his book *Wholeheartedness*. He states that it doesn't matter if you are young, old, married, have kids, etc.; overwhelmingly people feel like they do not have enough time to do the things they really want to do. I get it, I've been there and still have those days. But Chuck points us to a greater dialogue about our scarcity mindset. And I feel the need to point out a quick fact we can use to challenge our perception of busyness. If you look into statistics provided by organizations like the United States Bureau of Labor Statistics, the average American consumes roughly 3.8 hours of entertainment per day through devices like social media, Netflix or TV. If you don't believe that, just track and consider how much time you spend attached to your cell phone every day. So yes, we are busy, but not always for the best reasons.

Then again, stating a statistic like that won't mean much... until despair comes knocking on our door and puts our busyness into perspective.

Suffering is universal. It's not a matter of "if," but "when" – even if we try to live as though it is "optional." To understand another's cry means you have to let down your barriers that protect you from hearing it in the first place, like our tendency to avoid all things difficult. In the age of swipe left, swipe right, swipe up, swipe down, we can avoid the suffering of another in an instant. A video of kids dying in civil war? Nah. I'll take one of those cute cat videos. Oh, your boyfriend just left you? Sorry, I'm late for a meeting with a friend. You don't have any plans tonight? Unfortunately, I am going out with co-workers. We have lost our ability to become compassionate with others simply because we are not able to start at step one: listening. We are not typically even present in the very beginning to allow another person to share their cry in the first place. Then we are shocked to find out they are suffering at all. How many times have we said, "Well I had no idea..."

Let me be honest: if you are going to ask me how I'm doing while you're holding a cell phone, even if you have the best of intentions, *I'm going to lie to you.* I will do whatever it takes to get out of having any form of meaningful conversation because we live in a society where a text, an email, a phone call, a Snapchat or Tweet from another person is more important than making eye contact for any extended period of time. It is arrogant, it is rude, and it is utterly disrespectful to the person sitting across from us. The only message we are sending to that person is that at any moment, something more important than you might pop up on my electronic gadget and I need to be prepared.

I know, I've done it countless times to countless people. There is no such thing as multi-tasking human emotions. To hear the cry of another is to identify with their cry. Even if it is a cry of joy, you cannot be physically present if you are mentally somewhere else. Giving your attention, your eye contact and your presence, begins by listening.

Listening.

Listening is an act of love. To be heard is to be felt. To be felt is to be known. To be known is to be understood. When you can understand me and my pain, you can love me for all of me – the good and the bad. If I can trust you to listen, I can then trust you enough to share things that are hard to say. If I can trust you with things that are hard to say, I can share more of what it is like to be me. Then you can hear me, then you can see me, then you can understand me, then you can love me, in all my faults and follies.

CHAPTER 8 NOTES AND REFLECTIONS

What story do you need to share for someone to hear? Whose story do you need to reach out and ask permission to sit and listen? What distractions do you bring to the table that keep you from being fully present with that person and yourself? What portion of your 3.8 hours per day can you give to the person sitting across from you?

_____

_____

_____

_____

_____

_____

_____

_____

_____

_____

_____

9

EMPATHY:

I feel your cry

"Don't be afraid of sharing your vulnerabilities. Vulnerability doesn't make you weak, it makes you accessible. Know that your vulnerability can be your strength."
– Keith Ferrazzi

It was in that moment that time stood still.

I was a senior in high school and I had a struggling relationship with my father. For much of my adolescence, he lived a 14-hour car ride away which made it hard to maintain a deep relationship. We also didn't have an active father-son relationship. Being 50 years older than me and never taking care of his health, there was never any "playing catch" or going for a hike. Actually, most folks confused me as his grandson... which he never minded and used it to trifle for an extra discount at restaurants. He was going through his third divorce so stress was high and a blood clot in his leg rendered him unable to walk more than 50 feet at a time without enduring excruciating pain. He had known about it for two years at that point and had refused to have the surgery done or to even give up smoking. I begged and prodded every time we spoke but he always responded with, "Soon son, I will get it done soon." I slowly came to terms with the reality that my father would not be around for much longer.

I had hundreds of Mondays in school settings that have faded away from memory, but I remember every detail of this one. Sitting in the computer lab working on a book report, I was startled when the announcement over the PA asked me to come down to the office. You know that feeling when your gut falls through the floor? I grabbed my bag and walked to the other end of the school which felt more like a cross-country hike. I tried to build up the courage to hear what was waiting for me as I rubbed my hands over and over again on my pants trying to get rid of the clamminess in my palms. I think a part of me knew what was waiting for me since

I had been secretly anticipating this call for some time now and I couldn't quite figure out if that was making it better or worse. I made it to the office to find out my father was in the emergency department at a hospital in Saginaw. I hopped in the car with my brothers and we drove north in what would account for the most silent car ride the four of us would ever have together. There was no use avoiding the anticipatory anxiety – ninety minutes of distress gazing out of the car window mentally creating different scenarios of what was waiting in the emergency room.

Two hours later, we were speaking to my godmother who had brought my father in to the ER. She was hysterical and her words could barely escape through her tears. The nurse behind the desk cleared us to walk through those big double doors into the back rooms where the doctor was waiting for us. I remember him telling us to brace ourselves because my dad was not going to recognize any of us. I entered the room to see my father flailing about on the bed. He was terrified despite the fact that the staff were doing all they could to keep him calm. It all seemed surreal – I realized that my father had no ability to comprehend who we were or what was going on.

And then it happened.

His soft brown eyes had all but disappeared in the black darkness of his dilated pupils. Our eyes met and I could feel his sight piercing directly into me.

He ceased moving.

I froze.

Time stopped.

If the clock was ticking or anyone spoke, I could not hear it. All I could see was the helplessness in my father's eyes, the sorrow, the pain, the sheer agony and terror. And then a sensation of warmth trickled down my spine vertebra by vertebra... a calm, a reassurance, an ambience of peace and serenity.

I don't know if I was giving it to him or if he was giving it to me. But in a tumultuous moment when all of life seemed to be spinning and flipping upside down, here it was, here was the tranquility in the chaos, the eye of the hurricane. I felt it, I sensed it, I heard it – everything was going to be okay. We had an eternity of conversations in a single moment and then he laid down his head, drifting off into the endless sleep of a coma, and life would never be the same again.

They say even light can't escape a black hole. It appears to be massive, but the black hole itself is actually an infinitesimally small point that can weigh as much as a billion suns. That's the closest comparison I have to the weight I felt when staring into the darkness of my father's eyes. It is not easy or comfortable to put into words and a part of me has always tried to protect myself from ever feeling that again.

Though I didn't know it at the time, it was the last real moment of connection I would ever have with my father.

I spent nearly a decade avoiding even the idea of discussing that moment with anyone because it felt like the safest thing to do. If we hide, if we seek protection behind our smartphones and the four walls of our home, then we don't have to "feel" the pain of the world, the pain of another, and most importantly, we don't have to feel our own pain. The result? The endless pursuit to avoid all pain allows the pain to end up controlling our lives, leaving us helpless in the end. Compassion is intentional, compassion takes time and energy, compassion takes empathy. To succumb to the reality of your own pain allows you to be present with the pain of another, *to feel their cry.*

Remember step 1? Sympathy takes time and it takes attention. You must stop what you are doing, push aside the distractions, and be present to listen to the cry of another. Empathy, on the other hand, is more than just listening; it is vulnerability to its core. In order to really engage the joy and sorrows of another, you must feel their cry. Now this does not translate into a ceaseless quest to take on all of the world's pain. No, because then you'd hardly be able to get out of bed; trust me, I tried that once and it didn't end well. Instead, empathy is about connecting with the pain of another that enables us to connect with the pain with which we are struggling in ourselves.

We've all watched a movie that made us cry – the love story that didn't turn out, the dog that didn't make it, the child that passed away. Before my father died, I prided myself for not crying; I viewed crying as a form of vulnerability and weakness. Sad movie? Choke it back. Friend crying? Choke it back. Sitting at a funeral? Choke it back. I drank all those nights after he died because it was the only way I knew how to let my guard down enough to actually express emotion. Being drunk was the only way I could justify sobbing myself to sleep.

In the years after, I found myself becoming more and more emotional. Did I cry when watching *The Notebook* when they died together in bed? You bet. I cried when I had to put my dog down, at funerals, even when I got dumped. Before long, it didn't take much to make me cry as though I was making up for all of the years of holding it in. Why? Because the movies, the stories, the funerals were tying into a pain that I felt. Pain that I had not grieved for, or had refused to grieve for: regrets, moments of remorse, mistakes and everything I was bottling up trying not to face.

Our culture paints women as emotional and men as cold and distant. It is infuriatingly disappointing in the strictest sense. Expressing emotion, crying, and feeling are essential to the foundation of compassion. It takes strength to engage your emotions and it takes even more strength to be accessible and share them with someone else. Have you ever divulged a painful story to someone or cried in front of another person and they sat with a cold face without expressing any emotion? How did that make you feel? It can be terrifying.

When someone decides to share their sorrow with you, it is one of the most vulnerably engaging acts we can experience. To have empathy is the most respectful thing we can do in return. To feel sad with another who is sad, to cry with another who is crying means that we're getting in touch with the pain within and saying, "You are not alone, I understand, I am here with you." In our moments of pain and despair there is just one thing that feels worse than the pain itself: isolation in our grief. The capacity for human connection (often through empathy and empathy alone) can be the only thing standing in the way of facing grief or being overcome by it.

But connection is not the only thing at stake here.

I often lead group retreats to create safe spaces for folks to process through the pain of their stories and realize how they can be more intentional with their lives moving forward. It is one of the most rewarding experiences to see men and women come to life when there is an environment conducive to not only engaging their vulnerabilities, but peers willing to sit with them and engage in that pain. One of the most profound takeaways I've learned over the years is that you cannot suppress pain, despair and heartache without suppressing joy as well. My friend Josh Bishop, a PTSD and trauma therapist, explained it best; "emotions are like a radio knob, you turn down one, you turn them all down." Connecting with the pain of another is not an attempt to make yourself sad, on the contrary, it is fundamental to experiencing more joy.

My longing is that you are not overcome with the fear of what this work may entail, but that you may see the joyous gifts waiting for you on the other side. As the saying goes, everything you want is on the other side of fear...

CHAPTER 9 NOTES AND REFLECTIONS

How do you avoid empathy? How do you engage in empathy? What outlets do you share with others to create safe places to engage vulnerability? What outlets do you need personally to engage your own vulnerability?

_____

_____

_____

_____

_____

_____

_____

_____

_____

_____

_____

_____

10

SOLIDARITY:

I join your cry

....

"We are all beggars, it is true."
– Martin Luther (Circa 1546)

....

I
f I ask you to paint me a picture of a "beggar," I don't doubt your mind would automatically see someone holding a cardboard sign asking for spare change. Yet we all come into this world crying, reaching out for the mother who gave birth to us in the first act of begging for warmth, for shelter, for food and connection. But it doesn't stop there.

I remember the first time I got food poisoning like it was yesterday. A simple chicken and broccoli dinner that would ruin broccoli for me for the next decade. The tingle in the stomach that turned into a cramp and the lump that started to form in my throat. Then the slowly rising tide of pain and nausea accompanying the dark reality of what was about to come. The hours, the all-night marathon of deciding whether it is best to be sitting on the toilet or kneeling in front of it. It's excruciatingly painful in between heaves, gasping for air. It leaves your whole body in agony as though a drill sergeant made you do sit-ups for twelve hours straight. Then the dehydration comes because you can't keep any fluids down, followed by a fever. A small form of delirium takes place. When you are sick, you can take medicine to relieve some of the symptoms. When you have food poisoning, you can't so much as take a sip of water let alone take an ibuprofen without it coming back up. You can't stop it, you are at the mercy of your body, and without a doubt, begging for it to be over.

I have pleaded with my parents as a child, pleaded with teachers when I forgot my homework, pleaded against the forces of nature when experiencing turbulence on a plane, pleaded with bosses when I've made mistakes, pleaded with a lover not to leave, I have begged God for more time and begged loved ones to not pass away. When I was doing well financially and professionally, it was easy to separate myself from the "beggars." I was the one who helped those in need, not the one who needed help. It kept a safe barrier between my superior ego and the rest of the world – between those who need and those who provide the needs. That is, of course, until it was gone, all of it: my health, my relationships, my businesses, my wealth and the power, the money, the success, the ego, the courage, the strength, and the independence that came with it.

Then it was me who was begging once more.

That's why losing *everything* can be such a gift, if we let it. But it is also why losing *anything* can also be a gift. It reminds us how much we need others, how interdependent we actually are. Life can be really, really hard. There is no denying it. Losing a loved one, divorce, job loss, natural disasters, car accidents, you name it. We don't even have to lose it all to be consumed by fear or to find ourselves in a momentary state of desperate need. We think we are the kings and queens of this world and in control of our own lives. But it can take something as simple as bad weather on a plane or some undercooked chicken to bring us to our knees. And in those moments, it reminds us how much we actually want to change.

"I didn't have a map of who I was, I had to shed layers
of who I wasn't to discover who I am."
– Chelsea Nielsen

I have spent nearly two years in a season of scarcity. I've gone from being the king of my own empire, wealth, businesses, non-profits and save-the-world missions to being poor in finances, poor in health, poor in relationships, poor in love, and poor in my faith. One of my biggest takeaways in living with this season of scarcity is it taught me to realize the abundance I already own. To ground myself in how much I have to offer my community in times when I may not physically have much. I still have my presence, my ability to love others well, and my ability to care for another in need as well as myself. That season lasted almost two years and, in some ways, still exists.

Many friends, like Chelsea, shared countless hours with me bestowing their wisdom upon me in those two years showing me how to transform my perspective into the abundance over scarcity mindset. I'll never forget the day I was interviewing Amanda Gilbert from Henna Crowns of Courage where she shows the inner beauty of kids and women with cancer by painting henna crowns on their bare heads after the chemo and radiation had removed all of their hair. While my faith had been predetermined on my ability to produce results for the world, Amanda stopped me in my tracks when she reminded me that, "You cannot serve both God and money" (Matthew 6:24). I've heard the verse dozens of times, but on that afternoon, it left me dumbfounded in my vision of scarcity. I didn't even realize how much my faith was dependent upon financial success.

Scarcity left me constantly stressed, anxious and angry, wondering why I couldn't get out of this hole when the entire economy seemed to be booming. Scarcity kept my mindset constantly longing elsewhere to define my value in jobs, relationships, wealth, health and resources. Yet in grounding myself in all that I already possessed, I was able to bring a new perspective into the world in order to let go of my fears, my outcomes and my expectations. For those who joined my cry and showed me another way, I was able to faithfully pass that knowledge on to others. They showed me how connected I am – not to what resources I attain in the world, but to the complex web of life as a whole. To join the cry of another releases me from the story that's all about "I" and places me into the greater story that is all about "us."

Connectedness, not autonomy, is woven into the foundation of the universe. I want to give you a very concrete example as I am a science nerd and I'm fascinated by the complexity of the interconnectedness of our ecosystems. One of my favorite case studies in college revolved around the resuscitation of Yellowstone National Park. Let me share the 30-second version for all my friends who may not be science nerds. After re-introducing wolves back into Yellowstone, the elk and deer population began to come back under control, which allowed vegetation and trees to grow in the valleys once more. This new foliage created habitat for song birds to return. The wolves also reduced the coyote population which allowed rabbits, mice, weasels and badgers to flourish once more. The abundance of small game meant the revival of the hawks and eagles. The growth of vegetation and trees allowed the beavers to rejuvenate and provided adequate food for the populations of the bears to increase, and the ample roots from all of the new growth ceased erosion along the river banks. The decrease in erosion cleaned up the waterways and stabilized the river patterns allowing them to slow down and meander once more.

In a nutshell, the introduction of a handful of wolves changed not only the animals in the ecosystem, but the physical landscape itself. That is how interconnected we are as humans, even in our concrete jungles. You do not eat, sleep, or breathe without the interactions of other organisms. The trees and ocean filter the air we breathe, bacteria and fungi make nutrients available in the soil for the plants to grow so we can eat, ocean currents create weather patterns so we can have rainfall, the sun is the basis of every form of energy we use. To bring it full circle, this is the foundation of interconnectedness that exists before our Chapter 3 & Chapter 7 discussions on needing help and finding a purpose. This is the root of it all, the foundation before people can build the houses and teach at schools and make cell phones and install Wi-Fi and sew clothes and sell clothes and mine and harvest and create and design and imagine and provide...

Infinite interconnectedness.

We are full-heartedly dependent upon the resources and the sharing of those resources with other people. To respect community is to respect the fabric of what makes you, you. Therefore, when one element is suffering, the whole system is ultimately suffering. You cannot remove the wolves without hurting the rivers and the songbirds because you cannot harm one part of the ecosystem without simultaneously affecting all parts of the ecosystem. It is obvious then to see that the suffering in one person is the suffering in all of us.

To join the cry of another is actually to join the cry in yourself.

In solidarity we acknowledge that we are all one, that we are all interconnected, and we all need each other; it is true, we are all beggars.

To quote Karen Armstrong one last time, "Our pain, therefore, can become an education in compassion." When you are hurting, when you feel the sting of loneliness, do you at some point not long for the companionship of another? Do you not long for somebody to care about your pain, to acknowledge your pain, or at the very least to make note of your existence and to say that you matter too? Why else would you complain to a friend about a fight with your spouse or a problem at work? I don't believe it is because you just need to vent. What is the point of venting if it isn't to share the pain, anger and frustrations of a situation? If you truly didn't need anyone then why not talk to a lamp instead? A lamp might honestly be better at listening and is certainly less likely to interrupt or give bad advice.

We rally behind our loved ones when they are hurt, we attend the funerals of lost ones, we share the pain and frustrations with those we hurt and those who have hurt us, we vent, we cry, we complain, we scream, we hide, all because we long for the interconnectedness of compassion. It is a reflection of our longing for love the minute we are born into this world crying and screaming. It is the vitality of human existence to say that you matter, your pain matters, and it does not define who you are.

Let me say that again: you matter, your pain matters and it does not define you. Whether we are together or a thousand miles apart, I am in this with you, we are in this *together.*

As we wrap this chapter up for those of you who are going back and forth on anything I just said, I want to point out one obvious thing here. This whole concept does not mean that we are lost in a constant haze of despair to all of the world's problems. We can only be present with what is in front of us in the present moment. It reminds me of Archbishop Desmond Tutu talking about the Dalai Lama. He says the Dalai Lama can be sharing a tear with one person lost in grief and 30 seconds later be rejoicing in laughter with the next person. He is completely and utterly present in the very moment, meeting whomever, wherever they are.

So I ask you again, if and when you are mad/sad/scared/hurt/crying, what is it that you wish from another? Do you wish to be left to waste by yourself or do you wish for solidarity in your pain? That is the essence of how our pain can become an education in compassion. It comes when we can realize that we do not long for suffering, although we still know it is inevitable and in that suffering we long for others to be compassionate toward us. In following the golden rule of life, "Do unto others as you wish they had done unto you," that is our lesson in which we no longer look upon others and their pain with separation or barriers. Instead, we join in solidarity with their cry to say that you too matter, and so does your pain, regardless of all the mistakes we have all made in this life.

Aaron Niequist puts it beautifully in his book, *The Eternal Current.* The river has been flowing since the dawn of time and we get to choose whether or not we want to wade in: "The invitation is participation." To have sympathy is to listen. To listen is to understand. To understand is to have empathy and to have empathy is to be vulnerable. To be vulnerable is to feel the pain of and with another. To have solidarity is to join their cry. To join their cry is to realize that their cry is your cry. When we see the cries of all of our community, we are then called to action to say, "This isn't the only way."

CHAPTER 10 NOTES AND REFLECTIONS

Define interconnectedness for you and your life. What does it take to bring you to your knees? What does it take for you to join the cry of another? What does solidarity with another person physically look like for you?

_____

_____

_____

_____

_____

_____

_____

_____

_____

_____

_____

_____

_____

11

GENEROSITY:

I act on behalf of your cry

*"When the whole world is silent,
even one voice becomes powerful."*
– Malala Yousafzai

Friends, we have made it to the final piece of our four steps to compassion as we conclude with action. Action is, of course, the last thing to take place. Too often and without thinking things through, we skip straight into the idea that we need to act, to resolve, to serve justice. We don't give things proper time to heal or to even understand the situation in its entirety in the first place. How can we ultimately serve another person if we don't know, in whole, what we are attempting to serve them for? Action comes in many forms, and the spectrum ranges from simply loving a person well to fighting systemic injustices. We'll discuss both ends of the spectrum, but, for starters, if I ask you to describe to me what "action" looks like, I think that you will, at some point, paint me a picture of righting a wrong or balancing the scales of justice. So let's begin there.

Have you ever spent time in a foreign country, with a language you couldn't speak, while a group of strangers pointed AK-47s at your head? I had the good fortune of spending a weekend with Jer Swigart, co-founder of the Global Immersion Project, an organization dedicated to restoring peace in the world through training people in how to engage all of the division and hostility. The stories seemed fictitious, beyond Hollywood, surreal at best. How did a young kid in seminary end up brokering a peace deal between tribal leaders in a 30-year civil war while sitting next to a United Nations General in Northern Pakistan to save the lives of thousands? Did I mention it was in the hometown of Al-Qaeda while we were in the middle of a war with them four years after 9/11? And this all because he felt called to go and help in the midst of a humanitarian crisis from a 7.6 magnitude earthquake that decimated entire towns. Then you see the pictures and try and pick your jaw up from the floor (I know, I know... I'm going to leave you hanging on that AK-47 part, but he tells the story much better than I would).

One of the most striking things I took away from Jer's book, *Mending the Divides,* was the difference between peacekeepers versus peacemakers. Peacekeepers use force to subdue – think authoritarian regime, law and order, republican and democrat. One side is in power, another side needs to be put in their place. Peacemakers are about engaging all voices for a greater understanding. To see your enemies, to hear their pain and story, to put aside all of your judgments and accusations and choose to work together for long term solutions. It's a subtle difference in wording, but it bodes a profoundly different impact.

Now we don't have to be in war torn areas to act as though we are the all-powerful-authoritarian "peacekeepers." We can do that simply through our judgments and biases. We love reality TV, and drama, we are addicted to the news. It is always an "us versus them" battle. The endless tirade of judgments points to the pitfalls of society and our ideological or religious beliefs against anyone whom we perceive as being *different from us*. It is one of the largest failures of all civilization. To perpetually point the finger, to judge and criticize, is an outward expression of the depth of our own inward helplessness.

We feel inferior or insecure about our pain, anger and issues and we decide that the best perceived path forward is not to own our shortcomings, but to attack the pitfalls of another. Our actions become noxious to our life and those around us. It's another way to keep the "us versus them" battle going and our culture appears to be on a hell-bent tirade to never stop judging each other. We've gotten so used to doing it and hearing about it that it becomes commonplace every time we meet up with a friend or colleague to share our gossip.

Negating the pain and struggles of another person, to say they deserve to receive such treatment is merely a reflection of our own intentions to dismiss the pain and struggles in ourselves. The other day I found myself judging the shopping cart of a stranger at the grocery store. Why? It doesn't matter if it's a diet, job, outfits, parenting, statements, actions, relationships, co-workers, family – we can always find someone about whom we can say, "at least I'm not *that* bad" (as though I've never eaten a piece of candy in my life). To dismiss or devalue another is our attempt to elevate ourselves when we feel like we have no control over anything else. What led me to justify judging that person's shopping cart? I would tell you it had nothing to do with insecurities, but instead I was fighting for health, food systems, the environment, etc. All true and good things. But if I met every stranger from a place of love and grace, I wouldn't start with judgments no matter how much I disagreed. What was *really* going on one layer deeper? Well I've been battling various illnesses for eight years now and I'm sick and tired of being sick and tired. I just want to be able to enjoy a beer and a piece of pizza like a normal American and I can't. I know when I'm off kilter because when I am sound and whole in myself, I never – ever – waste precious time in my life doing something as impractical as judging another's shopping cart (or judging anything about their life for that matter).

Even if we don't think we are projecting our insecurities, we will still try to justify our criticisms and judgments because we falsely believe that we have the superior knowledge or we know what is best and it is up to *"me"* to solve this. Judgments with a lack of understanding only leads to more division. No matter how deep you want to look at your criticisms, when you combine any of these unhealthy trains of thought with action, the water gets muddy fast. Becoming a peacekeeper won't bring more health and vitality for greater change into this world – we need peacemakers.

Since action can be so complicated, I'd like to break it down into a couple of pieces and the corresponding pitfalls of each. For example, when you begin to act on behalf of the cry of another, it must be geared toward greater peace. There is no true justice in the balancing act of who owes what to whom and who deserves what. No one deserves suffering, no one deserves a life of pain and sorrow, we all deserve love and forgiveness, as hard as that can be to see sometimes. To begin the journey of serving alongside another is not about righting what is wrong. If the outcome is to even the scales then there will never be an end to the pain because you are going to walk down the road of revenge, not compassion. You will not justify that person's suffering by trying to place that suffering onto another. Isn't that the definition of civil war if we are all in this together?

I know what is likely going through your mind right now. Am I advocating for an unrealistic agenda of a utopian society? Am I advocating to open all the prison doors while promising that everything will be ok? No and no. As an alternative, I am asking us to collectively look at our current situation. I am asking us to look at all of history and to admit that we need to learn from our ancestors and to say perhaps we can do better (or maybe even *a lot better*).

Our current use of justice and worth is flawed at best. Justice would have meant sending those young men to jail in South Africa for the murders they committed. If you commit a crime you pay a price, yes. But justice will not stop the violence, it will not stop the hate; on the contrary, it can enable it. The United States holds the highest incarceration rates per capita in the entire world. It is a for-profit entity and business has been increasingly booming for decades. Books like Michelle Alexander's, *The New Jim Crow*, have challenged many of my preconceived notions on how we have the current justice system in place and how it affects our perceptions on due process. Not only how flawed it is and how colorblind we have become, but also in uncovering the knowledge that leads to a greater understanding and more effective action. One of my favorite quotes from her book:

> "Martin Luther King Jr. called for us to be love struck with each other, not colorblind toward each other. To be love struck is to care, to have deep compassion, and to be concerned for each and every individual, including the poor and vulnerable."
>
> –Michelle Alexander

Wars, literally or metaphorically, rage because one person decides they have value and worth over another and that they are going to seek the power and dominion to prove that. Eventually that person or group is defeated and oppressed and the oppressed will eventually rise to power and become the oppressor. This mentality resulted in the deaths of over 1,000,000 people in only 100 days during the Rwandan Genocide. If you need an easier context, think Republican versus Democrat where we will tarnish entire relationships and ruin Thanksgiving tables because of our clashing political beliefs. But it isn't just war and politics, it is how we engage our relationships, our families, our work life – we are addicted to a tit for tat mentality.

It's time we stop attacking the symptoms of our issues and begin looking at root causes. It's time to ask – constantly and persistently – the most challenging question: "How did we get here?". What drove that person to commit that crime? What causes a parent to yell at a child? What leads a friend to gossip about another friend?

Consider your relationship with yourself. If you get a headache, what do you do? Motrin, Tylenol, aspirin; you pop a pill. You don't stop to ask yourself why you have the headache in the first place. Instead, you automatically chose to address the symptom. The headache is a warning sign your body uses to tell you that something is wrong. Political feuds are a sign that something is wrong. Anger, envy, greed, wars, famine, homeless youth, sex-slave trafficking, racism, sexism, poverty, 40 million Americans who suffer with anxiety and depression... *these are all signs that something is wrong!*

Ironically, there is statistically no shortage of resources to solve many of the issues of the world. For example, in America we tend to blame the world's famines on overpopulation, but we feed more calories to our livestock and throw more food away in just this country alone than would be needed to solve all of world hunger. What we are lacking is a change in our perception. We must evolve the direction, contemplation and basis of our generosity upon a new way of thinking – not in justice – but in creating a new definition for worth.

So how do we become *peacemakers*?

Generosity is not about revenge; generosity is about love. It is about opening our eyes to the greater humanity we all share. It's about letting a person know, not just in words, but through physical actions that they are indeed loved, that they have worth, and meaning, and that there is another way – a more compassionate path through life. The offenses laid against them, the atrocities they have been through or committed themselves do not have to define them. The question becomes, how do we see it? (If you want a challenging discussion on the topic, I suggest watching the documentary *As We Forgive* on the reconciliation of the Rwandan Genocide.)

There are times when I get lost in my smallness in the enormity of the world's problems and wonder who I am and what the point really is. I have heard the pain of others, pain I could never explain, justify, or make sense of, and I've sent myself into an uncontrollable spiral of doubts on all matters of life. But I have never doubted the point of our existence on any level when I was able to be there for someone else. Sometimes I just really need the help of another to break me out of my narrow viewpoints on life. To realize that I get to – *that I am lucky enough to have the opportunity to* – play a small part in the reconciliation of bringing greater shalom and peace into this life. To get a taste of the Heaven I heard so much about when I was a kid and discover it not just somewhere I go when I die, but the gift in being a part of creating it here, now.

By now I hope you are asking a couple of really *good* questions like:

> *What can I do?*
> *How do I do it?*
> *Where do I do it?*
> *When do I do it?*
> *Why do I do it?*

By now you may also be asking a couple of really *hard* questions like:

There are so many problems in the world, how do I choose?

I'm just one person, what difference could I possibly make?

Life is already full, how can I possibly make room for more?

What knowledge and/or resources do I possess for change?

Sometimes it's the stories of the impossible that give us the courage to take the first step in trying to answer these questions.

Rick was born with cerebral palsy to Dick and Judy Hoyt. He would never be able to walk or move without a wheelchair and had complete dependency upon other people. Rick asked his father if they could participate in a fundraising 5k run to help another kid from his school who suffered from a spinal injury after being in a car accident. Upon crossing the finish line, he told his father that when they were racing, he no longer felt handicapped. That single sentence was the catalyst for over 1,000 races that the two of them would participate in – from 5ks to biking and running across the continental United States to seven full Ironmans! That means Dick pulled Rick in a raft for 2.4 miles of swimming followed by a bicycle ride for 112 miles and then pushed him in a wheelchair for a 26.2-mile marathon, consecutively, without stopping. Not once, but seven times.

The first time I saw the Team Hoyt video was in 2010. I had never run a 5k race or had even remotely considered a triathlon, let alone think to pursue either while simultaneously carrying, pushing, and pulling another human being. I live in a world where competition is everything. Society has constantly told me that if you aren't first, you are last. But that world doesn't exist for someone like Rick, nor does it even matter. I dreamed of the day when I would get to help someone feel alive and share that gift like Team Hoyt.

In June of 2017, I would get that chance. After suffering a complexity of health issues for years, I was finally seeing some progress. For the first time in more than five years, I was able to sweat. It was strange to be excited about something as simple as a bead of sweat, but it was a sign my health was improving. It also meant I could effectively regulate my body temperature. This allowed me to exercise more and more which was something I used to take for granted. One evening I was having tea with my friends Brooke and Ryan, explaining how exciting it was to engage in physical activity again, "Sometimes you really can't appreciate the ability to do something as simple as exercise until you physically can't." After recalling the memory of the Team Hoyt video, Brooke suggested I look into My Team Triumph; an organization dedicated to serving folks like Rick Hoyt. Persons with disabilities (Captains) get to compete in everyday races with the help of athletes (Angels) as though the Captains, not the Angels, are the athletes.

It was a beautiful June morning and I had hardly slept anticipating the 5 a.m. alarm to make it to my first 5k race. I remember a van pulling up to the race tent and my heart pounded as I heard somebody screaming. To my surprise, I discovered that a gentleman with Down Syndrome was yelling, not in pain, but in pure joy as he ran into a sea of red shirts, hugging and high-fiving all of the Angels. As the Captains began to arrive, it turns out I wasn't the only one who hadn't slept (although it turns out they hadn't slept due to excitement rather than nervousness). People from all walks of life had come together to serve folks with a range of disabilities for a united cause – generosity, companionship and joy. I had never been a part of such an astounding event that resounded with so much community and selflessness which simultaneously had the goal to serve people who would otherwise be left on the sidelines and told they could not compete.

Swimming was not in my vocabulary (open water swims terrified me), I had never biked more than ten miles, I had never run more than seven. After all of my health issues, at no point would I have considered the day I found myself able to pull a raft, push a stroller, or bike for miles on end. But when I put on that red jersey and found myself in that sea of red with voices cheering, laughing, smiling and crying, I found a new motivation. That summer I would continue on to race thirteen times, including four triathlons.

I first met Dakota at a 5k race. While he may have Cerebral Palsy, I never saw his spirits damped in the slightest. He was witty, loved to joke, and finished every race by crossing on his own two feet. On August 20th, we accomplished something I would have personally written off as impossible: a 1.2-mile swim, 56-mile bike ride, and a half marathon without stopping. After more than eight hours of listening to Dakota laugh and watching him smile, my teammates and I lifted Dakota out of his racing wheelchair, and together, step by step, crossed the finish line completing his first ½ Ironman. Eight hours of emotional exhaustion and physical pain ended in joyous tears with the sound of my daughter yelling "Daddy, Daddy!" and dozens of people cheering and clapping for Captain Dakota as he collapsed in celebration. My Captains and my team members inspired me to do the unimaginable, to go beyond limits and to unleash a strength which I never thought was physically possible for myself, let alone with another. I found such joy in serving a person who otherwise could not accomplish the feat on their own. And I couldn't have done it without the family of Captains and Angels who all believed I was capable of more.

This immense and incredible journey simply started with me asking some really good and some really hard questions. It started with me watching a story of the impossible and deciding to take a step in my own life. I've grown to love asking these questions. Making someone else's day makes me feel alive, it's addictive, it's contagious. To see a tear wiped away, even momentarily, and turned into a smile is the most beautiful thing I can think of. There's nothing like hearing a sigh of sweet and desperate relief. There's nothing like that infinitely long pause when my gaze is interlocked with someone else for an instant and I know that there is still good in this world and all hope is not lost.

In cultivating joy, we are not suppressing the pain and despair in life. We are not trying to balance out the scales or serve justice. My Captains would never be free from the pain of their disabilities. No justice would or could change that. But through their words and actions

I was taught that joy, not despair, can still have the final word at the end of the day and against all odds. They helped me redefine my own perception of worth and belonging. Most importantly, I couldn't have done it alone. We all have the ability to become peacemakers, to act on behalf of another no matter your circumstances or limitations.

Before we conclude this chapter, I briefly want to discuss the other side of the action spectrum; that of simply loving a person well.

> "We seek a compassion that stands in awe
> of what the poor have to carry, rather than
> in judgment of how they carry it."
> – Father Greg Boyle

Have you ever had a bad day and lashed out at an innocent person? Have you ever made mistakes that you would rather people simply not know about? Do you have burdens and pain from your past that rob you of joy to this day? Do they keep you from living and enjoying life to the fullest? Why give them that sort of power?

What if generosity meant simply letting go of the judgments of another and to stand by their side to let the world know they have value, too? I find that one of the best forms of generosity is not donating $20 to some cause or dropping off a coat to a child in need. Are these things important? Yes, that money could help feed that child and a coat may keep him or her warm and that is absolutely important and desperately needed. If you aren't at that level yet, it is most certainly ok to start there and the next chapter will be a short guide map summarizing how you can get started. But if you are there, I want to challenge you to take it a step further because financial contributions can still keep us removed from the situation at hand. We need to get engaged not only with our bare hands, but with our bare hearts. Our biggest act of generosity is taking the time to love – to love fearlessly and unconditionally without questioning what others may think. To pour out relentless love and compassion to all of those deemed "poor" in this life.

Sometimes one of the hardest parts about true generosity is the vulnerability that comes with it. To stand for another is to challenge something going wrong in society. The wrongness exists because others deemed it unworthy of time and resources. Generosity and vulnerability means you are going beyond a one time $20 donation to stand with a person or group of persons in order to say this isn't okay. I'm not implying you have to sell all of your possessions and move to a third world country and I'm also not saying that you can't or shouldn't – only you can discern your good and hard questions.

I'm simply stating that we've sat idle long enough. We've wasted 3.8 hours a day in mindless, numbing, worthless activities while a world of suffering waits for us to finish finding the right filter for our Instagram post and to look up from our phone. It's finally time for action.

What are we really saying with these actions? At the deepest level, we are saying this person or these people or this place or animal or environment does not *deserve* this; we're saying he/she/they/it is worthy. In the simplest of actions, a person may petition for change in a campaign of advocacy and educational awareness. In the strongest of actions, a person may place themselves physically in those shoes; building a water filter for Rwandans with 20Liters, blocking a bulldozer from building a dam with the women of Bosnia, helping a person who can't walk to get on their feet with My Team Triumph, mentoring a student once a week, and so forth... the opportunities are endless.

When we punish, suppress, and diminish parts of our world to say – you are below me, my standard of living, or my success – we spread the message that others do not deserve this quality of compassion. To engage in generosity with another is to say – if they do not deserve it, neither do I. *We all deserve it.* Remember, this is not about balancing the scales of justice or casting authority to determine another's worth. We have all made mistakes, we have all veered off the path more times than we can count, and yet still we stand. In our ability to stand we relinquish our rights to judge another for how they carry their burdens. Instead we stand in awe of it by helping them carry the burdens – by sharing the burden. Why?

> Because I'm not meant to carry all the
> burdens in life alone.

> Because I don't want to carry all the
> burdens in life alone.

> Because when I'm down and struggling,
> I want somebody to stand for me.

What organization or cause are you willing to fight for, not in the generosity of revenge, but in the generosity of love? Who's your Captain and who's your Angel?

CHAPTER 11 NOTES AND REFLECTIONS

How do you safeguard compassion to know that you are engaging others without conditions? In what areas of your life do you "keep peace" and in what areas of your life do you "make peace"? Who are your Captains and Angels? What actions beyond financial contributions can you take that engage you as a whole?

_____

_____

_____

_____

_____

_____

_____

_____

_____

_____

_____

_____

12

A CALL TO ACTION:

where rubber meets the road

I find the most opportune times to get involved are when emotions are running high and when I hear or see something that stirs my soul and calls me to act. If I wait too long, the feeling will fade away, I will return to the mundane schedule of my busy life, and the opportunity to be a part of something greater than myself will be once again lost. So below are a few steps I've outlined which you could take into consideration in the coming days and weeks to start asking and answering some good and hard questions in your own life.

1) What am I passionate about?

I remember by the time I graduated from college I was ready for a nervous breakdown just from trying to comprehend the sheer complexity and abundance of the world's problems. This was only alleviated when I realized the gift of humility: it's not up to you or me to solve them all. You have a unique set of characteristics and skills that can help solve a problem in a way that I can't and vice versa. What a gift, it means we get to work together! Moreover, there are no shortages of problems. Find ones that *call to your soul*, problems that enliven the innermost substance of your being. The more a challenge brings you to life, the more you will ultimately be able to make an impact.

2) What problems align with my passion? Research them on a local, regional and global scale…

Your problem may be a local issue like teaching local immigrant children how to read, or volunteering at the animal shelter. It may be a regional problem like creating healthy food systems for communities or addressing pollution in your city. It may be a global problem like working on anti-slavery issues in the clothing industry or aiding refugees in war torn regions of the world. Whatever the issue is, it likely plays a role locally, regionally and globally. I would wager that there are many organizations out there that need your help and have been waiting for you to call. If they don't exist, maybe this is your call to start one.

3) Where can I begin? Ask questions and listen...

Once you have determined "what" problem you are going to address and "where" you are going to address it, it's now time to sit with that community. Guided by the work we have done in this book, follow the road map to compassion. Let the person, people, thing, or place guide you in how you can best resolve the issue. Don't barge into a community with fresh fruits and vegetables when all they may want help with is finding proper transportation to work. Who are the leaders of the community? What organizations are doing similar work? What wisdom can they teach you? Befriend those you are trying to help, for the first act of compassion is to have sympathy and *listen to the problem* at hand.

4) Can I define the problem? Understand the problem...

Now that you are gathering data and asking hard questions, do you understand the issue at hand? If I asked you to give a presentation about it, do you know – in great detail – what it is you are trying to solve and how you may be a part of the solution? The second step involves understanding the problem through feeling the problem. How does this work connect with you and your life in a way that enables you to make the most significant impact? I promise you the work will become so much more meaningful when you aren't disconnected and isolated from the issues at hand.

5) How do I walk in their shoes? Find solidarity in the problem...

If you are going to fight against environmental pollution, don't drive a car by yourself all around town; lead by example and choose to bike, walk, use the bus, or carpool. If you are going to teach people how to cook nutritious meals, don't go to McDonalds for lunch. If you are going to engage a problem, live it out in your own life by joining the problem in the third step; solidarity. One of the best ways to truly connect with the problem at hand is to live it and experience it yourself. I'm not saying that you've got to throw all of your food away to understand food poverty and starvation, but if your doctor and health allows for it, perhaps you can try fasting to understand what restraint and hunger really mean. It will make your fight for change significantly more personable and relatable.

6) How can I take the first tangible step? Put your plan in motion...

Now that you have a clearer understanding about your calling to serve in this life – and you've researched it, learned what organizations are currently trying to address it or perhaps are starting your own, you've met with the afflicted, the leaders of the affected and those in resolution, and you've personally felt the issues at hand – it is finally time to act. I know it seems like a lot of additional work, but remember, we aren't just endlessly addressing the symptoms of the issues. We are making a long-term impact by chipping away at the roots and getting down to the cause. A word of advice here, don't go overboard and commit to ten things all at once because you'll get overwhelmed and you'll under-perform. Start by doing one thing really well. I know you are busy, we all are, but I also know you can allot one hour per month away from your social media and offer that hour to benefit your community.

13

COMPASSION IS WHO YOU REALLY ARE

"The problem with the world is that we've forgotten we belong to each other."
– Mother Theresa

I have sat at funerals only to hear the same words uttered over and over again: "she is in a better place," or "his pain and suffering is over." I have heard these phrases from the most devout people of faith and from diehard atheists. I also remember hearing the phrase, "There is no such thing as an atheist in a foxhole" when I was a kid. It would take me a long time to realize that in times of crisis or desperation, there are common themes that unite us all. Why? If some of us don't truly believe in a "better place," then why utter such a hackneyed statement?

Because when our facades are stripped away, we are left with the naked reality. In the moments when no one cares about our Facebook picture, who said what to whom, the size of our bank account or our home, how many friends we do or do not have, how far we made it in life or what our educational or social status is, then we are left naked. Naked and alone without our egos: looking up, looking out, wondering, hoping and longing for a greater sense of "why."

We all yearn to believe in something bigger than ourselves, something that provides a sense of meaning or purpose to life and to our personal existence. We are often our own worst enemies in failing to see the gift of life ourselves. We let awe and wonder fall short of deductive reason. We limit our own capability for the compassion and love we can share back into the world.

Every aspect of human civilization for thousands of years has pointed to some iteration of the golden rule. If we all followed it, all forms of war, hatred, violence, bigotry, and prejudice would vanish overnight.

Gone.

We know this, in the depths of our souls. Love and forgiveness are the source of all peace and harmony in this life, in our communities, and in this world. If we all lived from this place, no kid would go hungry, no one would take their last breaths alone, no one would feel the utter sting of isolation or unworthiness.

Love and forgiveness have a singular commonality. They are both expressed through compassion. Compassion touches on the very essence of our soul and it's what makes us who we really are. We are born out of original goodness, to be a source of light, to know that we are all deeply loved and hold an infinite ability to reverberate that love back into the world. We want to know that we too matter, that we have gifts amongst all of our imperfections, that we are worthy, that we are enough. Deep in the basis of our being, at the root of it all, compassion is who we really are. It is what makes Imago Dei so beautiful. The more we see that in ourselves, the more we share that message with those around us, the more it is felt, heard and seen in all forms of communication, and the more it reverberates back into our relationships, our families, our communities. Compassion, rooted in love and forgiveness, is the only thing that has ever changed this world for the better. It is the only thing that ever will. Why should we settle for anything short of compassion? Why should we let our lives be anything less than the greatness we already are and are destined to be?

We are all broken, we are all humbled, we are all weak, "we are all beggars, it is true," but we are also all filled with the divine light of the cosmos. It cannot be scientifically measured yet every person can feel it to their core.

You made it this far with me and I am forever grateful to have shared this time and to have initiated this conversation with you. Regardless of whether you agree with all of the ideas and content within these pages, with none of it, or likely somewhere in between, I'd like to leave you with a final and simple challenge. Start every day with one easy yet ever-so-powerful mantra:

Compassion is who I really am.

Try it and see where it takes you – I promise it has the power to change your life. Be who you are born to be, see the beautiful gift of life that is you in the mirror every morning when you wake up. Then share that light back to the world.

Grace, peace and compassion to you on this journey,

Thad

Resources

For information regarding future events, books or to request speaking engagements as well as for addressing any questions, comments or concerns regarding this book and its contents, please contact us. We appreciate your feedback to keep this conversation growing, evolving and moving forward in the world:

info@ChangingCompany.org
www.ChangingCompany.org

Resources:

The Book of Joy: Lasting Happiness in a Changing World
By Dalai Lama, Desmond Tutu, and Douglas Carlton Abrams

Braving the Wilderness: The Quest for True Belonging and the Courage to Stand Alone
By Brené Brown

The Eternal Current: How a Practice-Based Faith Can Save Us from Drowning
By Aaron Niequist

Hardwiring Happiness
By Rick Hanson

How to Love
By Thich Nhat

I Am Malala: The Girl Who Stood Up for Education and Was Shot by the Taliban
By Christina Lamb and Malala Yousafzai

May Cause Miracles: A 40-Day Guidebook of Subtle Shifts for Radical Change and Unlimited Happiness
By Gabrielle Bernstein

Mending the Divides: Creative Love in a Conflicted World
By Jer Swigart and Jon Huckins

The Most Beautiful Thing I've Seen; Opening Your Eyes to Wonder
By Lisa Gungor

The New Jim Crow: Mass Incarceration in the Age of Colorblindness
By Michelle Alexander

No Greater Love
By Mother Teresa

Quiet: Hearing God Amidst the Noise
By AJ Sherrill

Strength to Love
By Martin Luther King Jr.

Twelve Steps to a Compassionate Life
By Karen Armstrong

Wholeheartedness: busyness, exhaustion, and healing the divided self
By Chuck DeGroat

———————

Ashton Gustafson
www.ashtongustafson.com

As We Forgive (documentary)
www.asweforgivemovie.com

Chelsea Nielsen
www.theyogiyachtie.com

Crowns of Courage
www.hennacrownsofcourage.org

Leslie King; Sacred Beginnings
www.SBTP.org

Mary Johnson; From Death to Life
www.fromdeathtolife.us

My Team Triumph
www.MyTeamTriumph.org

Rob Bell
www.RobBell.com

Shane Claiborne
www.shaneclaiborne.com

Team Hoyt
www.teamhoyt.com

The Brave Women of Bosnia
www.patagonia.com/blog/2018/09
the-brave-women-of-bosnia

20 Liters
www.20Liters.org